6/11

Newcastle
City Council
Newcastle Libraries and Information Service

 **0191 277 4100**

Please return this item to any of Newcastle's Libraries by the last date
shown above. If not requested by another customer the loan can
be renewed, you can do this by phone, post or in person.
Charges may be made for late returns.

The Pocket Guide to Ballroom Dancing

Maureen Hughes

REMEMBER WHEN

First published in Great Britain in 2010 by
REMEMBER WHEN
an imprint of
Pen & Sword Books Ltd
47 Church Street
Barnsley
South Yorkshire
S70 2AS

ISBN 978 1 84468 082 5

A CIP catalogue record for this book is
available from the British Library.

Printed and bound by CPI Antony Rowe, Chippenham, Wilts

Pen & Sword Books Ltd incorporates the imprints of
Pen & Sword Aviation, Pen & Sword Maritime, Pen & Sword Military,
Wharncliffe Local History, Pen & Sword Select, Pen & Sword Military Classics,
Leo Cooper, Remember When, Seaforth Publishing and Frontline Publishing

For a complete list of Pen & Sword titles please contact
PEN & SWORD BOOKS LIMITED
47 Church Street, Barnsley, South Yorkshire, S70 2AS, England
E-mail: enquiries@pen-and-sword.co.uk
Website: www.pen-and-sword.co.uk

CONTENTS

Contents

For two very special people in my life:
Paula & Aisha

FOREWORD BY LEN GOODMAN

Photo courtesy of Len Goodman.

At the age of eight, I was riding my bicycle (on the pavement) when I saw a policeman heading my way on his bike. I turned around, trying to make my getaway, but he soon caught me up, having a far superior bicycle which had a double clanger gear change and racing tyres. Having stopped me, he started to chastise me on the dangers of riding on the pavement. I didn't like to tell him it was less dangerous for me than riding on the road. Anyway, my mum would only let me ride on the pavement. Having talked to me for ten minutes or so, I was about to take my leave when, as an afterthought, he asked me to empty my pockets. I only had two pockets in my shorts and from them I produced two conkers, four marbles, an apple (half eaten), three toffees (unwrapped), some bits of Meccano, a pen knife with a broken blade, a piece of string, four pence, half pence and a single piece of a jigsaw. Now, you may be wondering what this has to do with a guide to Ballroom Dancing but, just as the policeman couldn't believe how much I produced from my pockets, I couldn't believe how many facts Maureen Hughes has crammed into a Pocket Guide to Ballroom Dancing.

As soon as I started reading I warmed to Maureen when she revealed she started her dancing at the Court School in York whereas I started in 1958 at the Court School of Dancing in Welling, Kent.

I have, over the years, read many books on all aspects of Ballroom and Latin American dancing but Maureen's book is truly unique. It is crammed with facts, references and quotes which are absolutely fascinating to all fans of Ballroom and Latin American Dancing. I greeted the reading of this book as a chore but discovered it to be a joy. For anyone wanting to gain an insight into the history of Ballroom Dancing, the origins of the terminology, and the profile of many of the leading dancers and coaches, this book is a must!

ACKNOWLEDGEMENTS

There is nothing that can replace a family, and certainly no one who will give you that never-ending and unconditional love and devotion, and so to mine I want to say a big thank you. Thank you to all of you, for everything. I want to say sorry, too; sorry for not being there and for being so preoccupied for months on end in a way that I know only my fellow writers – and their families of course! – will understand. It's no excuse though, for I should have logged off my computer and logged on to all of your more important needs, because I love you all dearly.

To my friends too, who are not only consistent in their support, but helpful in so many ways; I want to say a special thank you to Jo for putting up with me for over fifty years, from childhood through to retirement. And thank you to Carol, who seems to know something about everything, which means that when there isn't a book on the subject then I just 'ask Carol'! Finally, a big thanks to my agent, Hilary at Straight Line Management, who I know has spent so much time chasing up people on the phone for me when I needed to do an interview. Mind you, she is rather partial to a good chat! And a final thanks must go to her assistant, Charlotte, for putting up with all those mundane jobs.

When writing this series of books, I made it my policy to contact anyone about whom I had written (or their estates in the case of the deceased). I then gave each individual the opportunity to amend, add or omit anything he or she wished from their particular piece. I did this because I wanted each and every one to be happy with the way in which I had portrayed him or her. The majority were delighted to be given the opportunity to vet the text and in addition many went to great lengths to make it read exactly as they wished, and so to all of you – I hope that you are indeed happy with the end result. I wasn't going to single anyone out here, but I must. I must say a huge thank you to the great and gracious Peggy Spencer, who went to so much trouble to ensure that I had all the information I needed, and to her daughter Helena too, who I know had a hand in helping out. What a wonderful lady Peggy Spencer *is* – for she is still actively involved in the world of dance, despite being in her ninetieth year; what an inspiration to us all! Thanks too to the lovely June Rycroft for her help; another lady who dances on whilst many of her contemporaries have hung up their shoes to rest their feet.

Thank you, to Mike Cooper, who was a great help to me on the Sequence Dance section and was so fascinating in his enthusiasm, and Mike Chadwick, who clearly loves his native Blackpool as much as a dancer loves the Foxtrot. Thanks too, to John Leach from Dance News Ltd., and to Derek Young of the Theatre Dance Council International who both went out of their way to help me. A special thanks to Paul Michael Jones (affectionately known only as PM), who is also the son of Stephanie Jones, my illustrator, and who acted as intermediary between us for no other reason than a son's love for his mother, which clearly shone through. The Jones Family – Stephanie, Steve and PM – as experts in the dance world – were also always on hand to answer my questions, for which I am grateful. And finally, thank you to Marcus Hilton, a gentleman who in the dance world has the label 'Mr Nice Guy' – and I soon learned why, for it was never too much trouble for him to help and advise, even when he was on the other side of the world!

INTRODUCTION

It was a searing hot Saturday afternoon in the early 1960s and there I was, standing in a queue on the staircase of the Court School of Dancing in my home town, the historic city of York, England, with my friend Stella Taylor where we were waiting to go into a Ballroom Dancing class. Most of my other friends thought I was decidedly odd, wanting to dance on a Saturday afternoon instead of meandering down Stonegate – Stonegate being 'the' street to be seen in on just such an afternoon in the swinging sixties; everyone who was anyone hung out in Stonegate, as it was teeming with hippies, the children of love and peace; it was also home to the obligatory sixties' coffee bar! But I didn't want to be in Stonegate; I wanted to put on my decidedly old-fashioned silver sandals and learn how to Quickstep. The evenings in York were the same, except in the evenings everyone 'hung out' at Ye Olde Starre Inn, which, of course, was in Stonegate too. I joined in then, but to be honest I guess I just wasn't cool, because I only joined in, in a vague and half-hearted attempt to fit in. You see, the truth of the matter was that I had other things on my mind, and what most of my friends didn't realise at that time was that dancing and theatre was my life.

Stella, of course, knew that I enjoyed our Saturday afternoons at the Court School of Dancing, but not that I belonged to a Scottish Country Dance Society, where I went each Monday evening, nor about the ballet classes – and she certainly didn't know that I saved up my pocket money to pay for private Ballroom lessons at another dancing school! In the fifties and sixties there were also those wonderful tea dances, and yes, I did partake in those too. I can admit it now, because my 'secret' is out, and anyway I have long given up any attempt at attaining even a modicum of street cred!

I can, now, with all the wisdom of age and experience, sit back and reflect on the fun and satisfaction I had when every afternoon, whilst on holiday in Scarborough, my mother and I went to the tea dance in the Ballroom on the promenade instead of sitting on the beach watching the boys go by – me, that is, not my mother. At that time this was certainly not 'normal' behaviour, for then it wasn't cool to be artistically aware or motivated. I carried on with my secret life for years, whilst still doing some of the other things which were considered more 'normal' and so allowed me to feel more accepted. I played squash twice a week, rode at the local stables every week and played tennis too in the summer months, but nothing compared to dancing and the theatre. As for the 'hanging out' thing, well, frankly I just didn't get it. It all seemed a bit of a waste of time to me! I mean, I still don't understand what everyone was actually *doing* when they 'hung out'; what were they waiting for when they stood for hours on end outside the local chippie?

Now, when it is okay to enjoy all things thespian or artistic, it seems a much more worthwhile approach to life. However, the fact is that I was born too soon and so my dancing life was a secret one, as were my regular solitary jaunts to the theatre. Oh how I wish I had been born when it was more acceptable for a teenager to be interested in all things theatrical; in fact not only acceptable but positively encouraged to the point that what was just a pastime in my day can now actually be a career. Of course, there were those, even then, who did make a career out of dance, but generally they were exceptionally gifted, and ballet then was the most accepted of the dance disciplines. Ballet and my natural physique though, as my family will vouch, would have made strange bedfellows even then, before the years took a hold. So I shall just have to be content with dreaming that had I not been born 50 years too soon – then maybe 'just maybe' I would have been a professional dancer – and not dwell on the fact that I probably wasn't good enough, or the right shape, anyway!

The most wonderful thing about the genre of dance that is Ballroom Dancing is that as a whole it seems to transcend all social and physical barriers as opposed to many other genres of dance. It did 50 years ago and it continues to do so today. Ballroom dancing was and is a social dance form in which anyone can partake and enjoy, as opposed to dancing to entertain the general public, as with most other dance forms. A Ballroom dancer does not have to excel, nor even improve for that matter, but merely has to enjoy the act of dancing. If a Ballroom dancer so wishes he or she can take qualifications, give demonstrations and/or even make a career out of it; but he or she can also have two left feet and yet still enjoy the social experience with like-minded friends and companions. Naturally, for those who wish to make a full-time career in this area of dance, then the usual high standards of physique, stamina and technical requirements are demanded of the dancer, for I wouldn't want to imply that any Tom, Dick or Harry can just join in and be an expert, for nothing could be further from the truth. But what I am saying is that any Tom, Dick or Harry can join in and just dance.

In recent years Ballroom Dancing has been given a whole new lease of life with that wonderful television series *Strictly Come Dancing*, which through sheer popularity is now known affectionately as simply '*Strictly*'. It's one of those rare 'I must stay in' cross-generation programmes that has taken the country by storm and brought Ballroom Dancing right back to the forefront. Long may it continue; long may anyone from the age of three to 103 enjoy Ballroom Dancing; long may the fat and thin, tall and short enjoy Ballroom Dancing; long may the fit and unfit enjoy Ballroom Dancing. It is a wonderful dance form for everyone – so get out there and *start dancing*!

Maureen Hughes

THOUGHTS TO INSPIRE
YOU TO DANCE

If you are reading this book, then it is doubtful that you actually need any encouragement to enjoy the art of dance, be it watching or doing. However, that does not mean that you won't enjoy browsing through these inspirational quotations, probably the most famous of which is the first.

'*Work like you don't need money,*
Love like you've never been hurt,
And dance like no one's watching.'

Irish proverb

'*There is a bit of insanity in dancing that does everybody a great deal of good.*'

Edwin Denby

'*We're fools whether we dance or not, so we might as well dance.*'

Japanese proverb

'*Dancing is silent poetry.*'

Simonides (556–468BC)

'*Nobody cares if you can't dance well. Just get up and dance.*'

Dave Barry

'*Dancers are the messengers of the gods.*'

Martha Graham

'*Dancing is wonderful training for girls; it's the first way you learn to guess what a man is going to do before he does it.*'

Christopher Morley, Kitty Foyle

'*Walk through life, run for your dreams and dance to eternity.*'

Anon

'*Dance till the stars come down from the rafters*
Dance, Dance, Dance till you drop.'

WH Auden

'*It takes an athlete to dance, but an artist to be a dancer.*'

Shanna LaFleur

'*You may walk with your feet, but you dance with your heart.*'

Anon

'*Those who can't dance say the music is no good.*'

Jamaican proverb

'*Those who danced were thought to be quite insane by those who could not hear the music.*'

John Milton

'*Dance is the hidden language of the soul.*'

Martha Graham

'*If you can walk you can dance. If you can talk you can sing.*'

Zimbabwean proverb

'*Never give a sword to a man who can't dance.*'

Confucius

'*I want to be liked*
To be loved and admired by you.
I want to succeed
In every way and in all that I do.

I want *to be happy*
Say goodbye to those tears.
I want *to feel safe*
As I banish all lingering fears.

I want *all these things with my heart and soul.*
But I need *to dance, for its dancing that makes me whole.'*

Anon

... AND SOME JUST TO MAKE YOU LAUGH

'*Dancing is a perpendicular expression of a horizontal desire.*'

George Bernard Shaw

'*He was a man who never let his left hip know what his right hip was doing.*'

PG Wodehouse

'*If dancing were any easier it would be called football.*'

Anon

'*The Three Styles of Tango:*
American Tango *is when you've just started dating, and you're flirting in an atmosphere of sexual tension.*
Argentine Tango *is when you've just started sleeping together and you can't keep your hands off each other.*
International Tango *is when you've been married for seven years and you're only staying together for the sake of the children.*'

Anon

AND FINALLY, FOR ALL YOU LADIES OUT THERE ...

'*Remember, Ginger Rogers did everything Fred Astaire did, but backwards and in high heels!*'

Faith Whittlesey

And as a final quotation to remember when your feet bleed and your limbs ache; when you feel that you will never be a dancer:

'Quitters never win and winners never quit.'

Catch 'em young and keep 'em forever. (Reproduced with kind permission of Mrs H M Elston)

Chapter 1

WELCOME TO THE WORLD OF BALLROOM DANCING

A SHORT HISTORY OF DANCE

Dance itself, in one form or another, has been around since time began, though unfortunately there isn't a series of detailed, chronological and historical facts to plot the evolvement and development of dance for the dance theory student. Dancing is, you see, part of the make-up of any living thing. Members of the animal kingdom have their own form of dancing that is a series of set movements they 'perform' in a given situation, to portray an emotion – courtship, for example – or perhaps to indicate an intention or even to stalk and kill their prey.

The human race is no different in this and has danced since time began. Prehistoric man, for instance, didn't have our complexities of speech to express his needs and emotions and so used movement as a vehicle to 'mime' what he would in later years be able to say. Fortunately for us, he captured these communicative mimes in a numerous series of drawings which depicted men and women dancing together. Examples of these can be found on the wall of a cave in Cogul, northern Spain. Further evidence of early dance can also be found in the writings of Homer (c1400–1200 BC), in which he describes circular and linear dances. So, as in the animal kingdom, the early form of dance quite clearly often had a purpose and was not necessarily merely the enjoyable pastime it is today.

As time progressed and the art of language developed the need for this form of communication was no longer necessary, but it refused to go away and die, proving that it is an intrinsic part of our very being, and so developed its place in our society as a part of our customs. In many areas dance then evolved into folk dances and so there remains a cultural root in various national dances of which nations are justifiably proud. Dances for the human species were often, and still are in fact, also a part of the courtship process as well being an important part of many religious ceremonies; historically, as well as courtship dances, there have been war dances, religious dances, and so on. One could even go so far as to say that dance is the core of the human species, existing as it did before speech, and that which pushed mankind forward in its quest for social development. Given this theory, then, it would seem that dancing is as basic to mankind as eating and drinking.

THE ARRIVAL OF BALLROOM DANCING

It is difficult though, if not impossible, to pinpoint the evolvement of Ballroom Dancing itself, at least as we know it today, which is as a separate art form to all other forms of dance. For you see, that's just what dance is, an evolvement, in that it evolved from many dances over a vast period of time throughout both the civilized and non-civilized world. As mankind and its world developed, so too did dance. Therefore, there can be no true creative history to this form of dance, but more of an amalgamation of various forms of dance from various cultures and international regions.

It isn't until the fourteenth century that we begin to find actual recorded evidence of specific dances, and it wasn't until the second half of the seventeenth century, in the days of the Minuet and the Gavotte, and also after Louis XIV had founded his Académie Royal de Musique et de Danse, that actual rules for each dance were laid down by members of the Académie. Furthermore, it wasn't until then that the five positions of the feet – which are still in use today – were formulated for the first time.

In 1812 we saw the first beginnings of modern dancing when the 'modern hold' made its debut with the Waltz, and what an outrage and scandal that caused, with men and women dancing so intimately – and in public too!

'No event ever produced so great a sensation in English Society as the introduction of the German Waltz. The Anti-Waltzing party took the alarm, cried it down, mothers forbade it, and every Ballroom became a scene of feud and contention, sarcastic remarks flew about, and pasquinades were written to deter young ladies from such a recreation.'
Anonymous 19th-century writer

Ironically since then many have laid claim to the Waltz being theirs and having evolved from their dance, their country and so on, but I am not even going to enter into that one as it seems a pointless exercise when nothing can be proved either way. As far as I am concerned, centuries ago the Waltz arrived, it stayed, and today it is still with us and showing no sign of leaving either. Doesn't that say it all?

The next development on the progressive road to modern dance was in the 1840s when the Polka and Mazurka arrived in the Ballrooms. Then a sort of stagnation set in until well into the twentieth century when a new and different way of dancing to Waltz music arrived on the scene; this was known as the Boston and appeased the younger generation who were bored with what was happening at that time. For a while there was little structure to dancing and a more rebellious approach prevailed. However, order was restored in 1920 when the first-ever committee of the Ballroom branch of the Imperial Society of Teachers of Dancing (ISTD) was formed, for it was they who codified a Modern Ballroom technique, which was based on natural movement and with the feet in alignment. Modern Ballroom Dancing, as we know it today, had finally arrived on the dance floor.

Now, I am not going to make any attempt whatsoever to teach you how to Ballroom Dance. I couldn't, even if I wanted to, and besides there are many excellent books out there to do just that, books written by true experts on the correct technique of this form of dance. *The Pocket Guide to Ballroom Dancing*, however, is in addition to those books and I hope full of interesting information and background knowledge, which it is intended will complement those excellent books on technique.

Until just a few years ago, to most people Ballroom Dancing was quite simply a case of 'slow, slow, quick quick slow' and a pastime thought of, in general, as for the elderly or perhaps the slightly more 'nerdy' of youngsters. Then along came that wonderfully successful TV show *Strictly Come Dancing*, where world-class professional dancers teach non-dancing celebrities how to 'do it'. And so it was that Ballroom Dancing came back on to the front line of recognition once again. Though I must be totally honest here, and say that it never really went completely out of fashion, for it has always been a part of the international dancing scene, but since *Strictly*, as it is now affectionately known, hit our screens Ballroom Dancing is loved and enjoyed by a much larger body of people, and more importantly by a much larger body of people across all age groups. And so as a result it is no longer considered to be for the older generation but has become 'hip', 'cool' and the 'in thing'. Every Saturday night for approximately three months of the year millions are nailed to their armchairs and glued to their TV sets, eager to see whether the soap star or rugby player can move with anything that vaguely resembles grace, as well as being enthralled by Ballroom Dancing.

Of course, as with all things, the style of Ballroom Dancing continually changes and will inevitably continue to do so, for that is the way of man and constitutes development and progress. So what we must accept is that what is popular and hip today will in fact be quaint and historic tomorrow! But one interesting fact is that Ballroom Dancing does seem to have some sort of amazing staying power and now it is almost necessary to be able to at least shuffle around the dance floor at least once, in movements that perhaps bear some resemblance to a Waltz, for we all at some point in our lives will be faced with dancing at the school prom, the first dance at our wedding or maybe just keeping the boss happy at the annual staff social. So in conclusion, we all *need* to be able to join in with Ballroom Dancing to a lesser or greater degree and as it is showing no sign of going away, then why not then follow the maxim: 'If you can't beat 'em, join 'em!'

Chapter 2

LET'S DANCE!

So now you're hooked and you have decided that the time has come for you to learn how to Ballroom Dance. A good reason all 'round for learning to dance is not only because it is a social activity but also because it is an excellent form of both physical and mental exercise. Life has changed beyond recognition in the past half century and it would seem that for many exercise is now not only a thing of the past but is also a 'chore' to be avoided at all costs, and so it is a definite plus to discover that not only is dance an enjoyable form of exercise but one that suits all ages too, and so can actually become a family pastime.

Of all the various forms of dance – of which, needless to say, there are numerous – Ballroom Dancing fits the bill on more than just the exercise front. As an example, for the very young it has the advantage of teaching a child to feel comfortable when in close contact with the opposite sex; for the more mature dancer then he or she can simply enjoy the act of being close up and personal, so to speak. Another plus side is that all dance is an excellent instructor in the long-forgotten art of posture. Ballroom Dancing has much to offer on a mental level too for it teaches self-discipline to all participants and an awareness of the needs of others. Of course Ballroom Dancing now exists and works under the name of 'Dancesport', which in itself indicates just how serious and recognised it has become throughout the world.

WHAT EXACTLY *IS* BALLROOM DANCING?

Well, using 'Ballroom Dancing' as a simplified umbrella term, it incorporates two main styles of dance, and there two parts which make the whole are: Modern Ballroom Dance and Latin American Dance. In the Modern Ballroom section we have the Foxtrot, Quickstep, Tango, Viennese Waltz and Waltz, whilst in the Latin American section we have primarily the Cha Cha, Jive, Paso Doble, Rumba and Samba. Of course, there are numerous further styles and dances on the peripheral of each category, which we will also take a look at in this book.

MODERN BALLROOM VERSUS LATIN AMERICAN

Most new dancers start off by taking classes in both Modern Ballroom and Latin American, which is quite sensible because how do you know to which you are best suited if you don't try them both? And then what generally happens is that you enjoy both and so continue with both which, unless you are going to be taking examinations or competing at a high level, seems by far the best option; variety is the spice of life; two for the price of one, and so on!

However, there is, of course, a difference between the two styles, which is – put simply, I suppose – that Modern Ballroom Dancing is elegant and sophisticated in style, whilst Latin American is a flamboyant and party style of dancing. Generally speaking, professional dancers, although technically proficient in both styles, do tend to specialise in either one or the other, although occasionally along will come a genius extraordinaire on the dance floor who will excel in both styles, as in the case of the iconic and mesmeric Marcus and Karen Hilton.

What then is the difference between Modern Ballroom Dancing and Latin American dancing? Well, it is not just the music, as one would expect, but it is the proximity of the dancers to each other which is the major difference. This is quite bizarre really, for one would expect that the dancers for the sensual Latin dances would be closer together than the dancers for the more, for want of a better word, aloof Ballroom Dances. But that is not the case at all. In the Latin dances the partners are much further apart than in Ballroom Dancing. Other than that, there are many similarities and a few more differences, for example:

The Hold
1. For Modern Ballroom a close hold is required.
2. For Latin American, dancers are permitted to let go of their partners.

The Style
1. Modern Ballroom is all about graceful motion and movement within the dance.
2. The style of a Modern Ballroom Dance is very formal and there is a sense that the partnership is as one body moving in harmony.
3. Latin American dances generally have a supporting narrative, which usually tells a sensual story.
4. Although the Latin American Dancers may move together it is with a more sensual freedom and individual rhythm.

Contact

1. In a Modern Ballroom Dance the partners do not look at each other.
2. In a Latin American Dance there is definite interaction between the two partners, who are in fact permitted to look at each other.

Now that you 'understand' Ballroom Dancing and the differences between the two integral styles you can learn a few basic steps and start dancing. It can't be that difficult, after all. Right? Wrong!

BEFORE THE DANCE

A few pointers then to keep in mind before you rush out and put on your dancing shoes. Do remember that, as with any art or sport for that matter, the preparation is a fundamental and important part of the whole. So, if anyone is thinking that this 'sport' is for them then there are things which need to be kept in mind, a few things to prepare, and then, following that – in my opinion anyway – a few terms with which it would be a good idea to be familiar; I always think that everything is much easier if the language used doesn't sound like a foreign language, but more of that later. First, you must *prepare* to dance, and remember that here the term Ballroom Dancing encompasses both Modern Ballroom and Latin American.

So, what is the first thing you need before you can dance?

Enthusiasm

It might sound a bit obvious, but believe me it's not, and so I say to you: 'Dance because you want to'; In fact, I would take it one step further – sorry about the pun – and say 'Dance not because you want to, but dance because you can't bear *not* to.' For you see, real enthusiasm will drive you through the pain barrier, oh, and trust me there will be pain, real pain; the pain of aching limbs and sore, even bleeding, feet; not to mention the pain of bruised egos as you stand on your partner's feet, trip over your own and end up in a heap on the floor, with everyone watching of course and then there's the greatest pain of all – humiliation. But none of this will matter because your enthusiasm will mask it all and carry you through. If, however, you are dancing because it is the 'in thing' to do, because all your friends do it, or because your mother has persuaded you that it is the ideal place for you to meet your future partner, then you will notice every little blister, not to mention suffer from high levels of boredom and frustration. But even if you want to be there with all your heart, you will still have to survive the mental torment that you will suffer, such as the excruciating feelings of inadequacy and incompetence which will rip you apart; the feeling that you are not good enough for your partner (now that is a really great way to destroy self-esteem); but even worse, if you can believe it, is the feeling that your partner is not good enough for you and is holding you back from reaching your full potential. Now, how do you tell someone that without a) sounding conceited b) destroying what was once probably a very good working relationship, if not friendship, and most important of all c) destroying someone else's fragile ego, hopes and dreams? Suddenly enthusiasm sounds like a lot of hard work doesn't it! And I can tell you that whichever of these is your problem and whatever decision you take in an attempt to solve your problem, you will not be free from the pain of mental anguish. Tell your partner the truth and you inflict pain upon him or her, keep it to yourself and you inflict pain upon yourself, and both decisions will inflict pain upon friends and relatives. So you see, there is no easy way out of this dilemma is there? All of this though can be successfully worked through, but only if you are brim-full of enthusiasm.

Enthusiasm in place then let's move on to *music*; you need *music* to dance ...

Music

Music for Ballroom Dancing is what is called *strict tempo*; it is called this because the speed of the music remains constant throughout the dance. In this section too we must be aware of the time signatures for each dance, for this tells us how many beats there are in a bar in each piece of music. Ballroom generally begins on the first beat of the bar, whereas Latin generally begins on the second beat of the bar. So much to know and remember and your feet haven't moved a step yet. But if you begin on the wrong beat, then the dance is over almost before it began! Of course, as far as the music is concerned there is still the *rhythm* to be taken into consideration too, for it is the rhythm which tells us the length of the individual notes and refers to the repetition of the accentuated beats. This in fact is the heart and soul of the music, and indeed of the dance, and so for that reason anyone who fails to keep in time with the music is said to have 'no rhythm'.

For now, however, let us assume that you do have rhythm – as well as *enthusiasm* – and so are ready to dance; so what you need now is a *partner*, for remember that Ballroom Dancing is a social dance form and therefore cannot be executed alone …

Partners

Having a partner is what makes Ballroom Dancing social dancing, and what can be more social than holding your partner close to you, whizzing gracefully around a room in beautiful clothes to sensual music? Then there is all the fun that comes with the preparation of your dances; the choosing of the music; the choosing of the clothes and the falling in an hysterical heap upon the floor when it all goes horribly wrong. None of this can either be done or enjoyed alone, for the preparation process is as much a part of the dance as the dance itself, and for both you need a partner. It is a very close bond which develops between dancing partners and so choose with care, for you may be two people, but you must dance as one. You don't have to love your dance partner as you would a marriage partner, but if you both have a deep and passionate love for Ballroom Dancing, then the rest will all fall magically into place and a great union will be born – and who knows, you might even find the love of your life too and have a dancing marriage, as many couples and indeed past champions have found!

So now there are two of you eager to start, but calm down, slow down and think about your *posture* – not to be confused with *poise*, which is a different thing altogether, though equally important for *posture* is the firm foundation upon which the technique is placed …

Posture

Two words spring to mind on this topic – horse and cart! So which comes first, in this instance – the horse or the cart; the good posture or the good dancing? Do you need good posture to be a good Ballroom Dancer, or does Ballroom Dancing improve your posture? I suppose it is a bit of both really, because you certainly cannot dance well unless your posture is good. In which case it stands to sense then that you should do all in your power to improve your posture before you begin to dance and then in turn the dancing itself will actually improve your posture even further. I think this might be a case of the horse sitting in the cart, don't you? If so, then who is pulling it? Well, enthusiasm, of course! You will discover though that those with naturally good posture do find Ballroom Dancing far easier than those

28

with naturally bad posture. Bad posture means you will be clumsy and probably kick and trample all over your partner, and not just his or her feet either, whereas good posture will mean that you will be naturally well balanced and therefore more likely to stay upright, which in itself is a distinct advantage for it means that you will learn and improve more quickly and your partner will have fewer bruises.

For the sake of kindness then we will assume then that both you and your partner have naturally good *posture*. So, *enthusiasm*, *partner* and *posture* in place, you are all set to start dancing. Right? Wrong again! For it is now that you need the *poise* ...

Poise

Dancers with a natural, graceful and beautiful poise are a joy to the eye, but for many this has to be worked on and acquired. Even though beautiful poise might come easily to some, it is still not something that is natural to most of us and so is an acquired art, or should I say technique. The Ballroom poise for the *lady* is a slight curve to the left with the head turned very slightly to look over the wrist to the left, whilst the head continues the line of the spine. For the *gentleman* the body should lean slightly forward. The weight of the body for both the lady *and* the gentleman should be on the middle to the front of the foot and never on the heels. In Latin American dancing, the bodies of both the lady *and* the gentleman should be poised very slightly forwards.

Okay, so you have now *enthusiastically* decided you just have to dance, you have found the *music* and chosen a *partner*; your *posture* is good and you are standing both correctly and in a *poised* manner. Each of you is raring to go and so surely now must be the right time? Yes? No! What are you going to do – both race off in different directions? No, of course not, for you must first take *hold* of your partner before you can dance ...

The Hold

Don't forget that although this is social dancing you can't simply grab your partner and go! The way in which you 'hold' your partner is an essential element in Ballroom Dancing that you must master before the actual dancing begins. I know – it's so frustrating when all you want to do is get out and boogie on that floor, but it's necessary, so this is how it's done for Modern Ballroom.

1. Both partners stand facing each other with the feet slightly apart.
2. The man raises his left arm, elbow bent, with his hand slightly above the level of his shoulder.
3. The man's right hand should then be placed just on or below the lady's left shoulder blade.
4. The man's right elbow should be picked up to match the height of his left elbow.
5. The lady must raise her right arm with elbow slightly bent as palm to palm she places her right hand in the man's left hand.
6. Next, the lady places her right hand on her partner's upper right arm – below his shoulder.
7. Partners stand in front of each other in a slightly offset position with the lady being slightly to the right side of the man.

(It is exactly the same hold for Latin American Dancing, the only exception being that it is not quite as cosy, as the partners stand about a foot apart.)

Finally you are ready to hit the dance floor, but the work isn't over, for you must 'keep your mind on the job' at all times. Keep heart though, for by now you should at least be standing on the dance floor, if not yet actually moving!

To gain the most you can from Ballroom Dancing and to achieve the highest possible standard in the area of PB (Personal Best), then you must work on your technique, understand it and then refine it. The eventual outcome being that you will always achieve your PB. Now, whether that is just having great fun with like-minded friends, entering competitions or becoming a world-class champion, is really immaterial, for you are dancing and at the end of the day that is all that matters. The basic areas of technique exist for all Ballroom Dancers and must be in place both before and during the dance to ensure an enjoyable experience on whatever level of competence. We have looked at what is necessary before the dance, so now let us look at what is required during the dance.

Almost ready to move now!

The Body
Dancers must, at the very least, start out correctly by standing in the correct position, for many would-be dancers look either stiff or uncontrolled. Those

who look stiff are generally standing with unnecessarily taut muscles instead of holding themselves naturally tall and proud. Those who have an uncontrolled look about their posture are generally standing with sagging shoulders, floppy arms and slack stomach muscles. The rules apply to both the man and the woman, who should in twin each stand tall and proud with their feet together. Heads, shoulders, chests and hips should be lined up over each other and over the centre of the foot; ribcages should be lifted and arms should hang down by their sides. The woman must not hang on to her partner, thus in effect weighing him down; neither must she hold on to him too tightly.

Once the correct starting stance is achieved then you're ready to go? Well almost! You now need to be a bit more specific and pay close attention to detail ...

The Head

There is also the position of the head to take into consideration. When learning to drive a car, you do not – unless you have a death wish – look down at your feet. It is exactly the same when learning to Ballroom Dance; you must not look down at your feet. Make this the rule from day one and there will be no problem, for it will come naturally to you from thereon. Remember that the head is heavy in comparison to other parts of the body and so if left to peer down at the feet then the balance of the dancer will be thrown out. Keep the head up and the eyes in a natural position; the gentleman's head should look straight over the lady's right shoulder, whilst the head of the lady should do the same and look over the right shoulder of her partner.

The final thing to think about before the feet start to move is ...

Lines

This is not as in line dancing, but body lines. Good dances can be ruined, slaughtered in fact, by marvellous dancers with poor body lines. All you have to do is think of it like this. The body is one whole machine and to work efficiently all parts must be used effectively. The arm, for example, starts at the shoulders and finishes at the fingertips; it does not end at the wrist thus allowing the hand to flop around all over the place; extend and control this entire limb, for even the nails are important – think about them too and you won't go far wrong. Dance with your entire body and not just with selected bits; extend and reach for the stars with every part of your being and you might just become a dancing star yourself one day.

Now you're ready, and you can finally start dancing! But remember that there are still some basic points that must never leave your conscious thoughts …

The Legs
These must not be allowed to have a mind of their own and must be controlled by the dancer at all times. There should be no apparent stiffness and they must in general display freedom from the hips and not from the knees, with a natural bracing and relaxing movement in each step.

Balance and Weight
This would suggest that the main objective is to not fall over and cause an obstruction on the dance floor. Now whilst this is always a good idea, there is a little more to it than that! Although this is, of course, a basic necessity and an essential, because let's face it who wants to be or who wants to watch someone who is all over the place – who can't stay upright in fact? But that aside, in dancing, balance and weight refers to elegance and ease of movement, for if the carriage of your weight is well placed then you will indeed remain upright, but more importantly you will achieve this with grace and style, and as a result you will be a pleasure to watch. But do remember that as you relax into dancing and feel more in control of your movements, then balance will become second nature to you, so don't worry too much about it. In our weight-obsessed society, it is interesting to note that weight also plays an important part in dance, but thankfully not in quite the same way!

I am sure that you will have noticed that the word elegance keeps cropping up, and that's because dancing is one of the most elegant sports of all time and this owes much to the correct distribution of weight. On this score, all you have to bear in mind is that the weight should be on one foot at a time only and the whole body weight should be transferred with each step, meaning that at no time should the weight be split between two feet. Good balance is actually only a matter of practice in walking correctly. Think about it, when you are walking along a street you would never push your feet out in front and then wait for your body to follow it now, would you? It is the same when dancing. You must carry your weight through with the moving foot. Good balance, therefore, will come naturally when the dancer is in control of his or her movements.

Footwork

Without feet there would be no dancing, as we know it, and certainly without *good* footwork there would be no *good* dancing. There are four parts of the foot used in Ballroom and Latin Dancing: i) toes ii) ball of the foot iii) flat of the foot iv) heel – and gradually, if you take lessons, then you will learn how and where to use each part, but for now the most essential part of footwork for you to remember and one that requires your attention is that of buying the correct footwear. As my own mother was forever telling me: 'Always buy good shoes and a good bed, for if you are not in one then you will be in the other!' Yet again proof that my mother was never wrong! So consult with the experts and buy shoes designed for the job, and then your feet can do the talking and walking – oh, and the dancing too!

Leading and Following

When I was at school, I was always chosen to be the man in dance classes, probably because I was tall and I suspect because I was also rather bossy too! (I went to an all-girls' school, you see). I actually found this to be quite unfair at the time and was convinced that it would be a handicap when I went to 'real' dances, but nothing could have been further from the truth, as I found that having been a man, so to speak, for the best part of my (dancing) childhood, I could fully understand what was expected of me and so let the man get on with his job of leading me around the dance floor. It's a bit like driving a car really – only one person can sit behind the wheel and decide which turning to take. So my advice to you, gentlemen, is to be confident and be sure of what you are doing, take control and make the lady feel safe. Ladies, don't fight the lead and let him take you around the floor. Of course, this all changes when you leave the dance floor, for gentlemen, your moment of supremacy is only about three minutes long, after which you must remember your place and do exactly as we ladies tell you.

Rise and Fall

The rise and fall is just as the words imply and for me epitomises the art of Ballroom Dancing. To see the dancers glide around the room as they 'rise and fall' is what gives this style of dance the graceful elegance for which it is both renowned and loved.

Sway

The sway is a quite simple, but very effective, movement and even more so when executed by both partners in total harmony. So what is it? It is the inclination of the body to the left or to the right, and here is the most important thing, it is the using of the *entire* body and ignoring the temptation to sway from just the waist up!

Dress

As a child, if I am honest, the glitz, the glamour and the beautiful sequined dresses were initially one of the major attractions that drew me into the world of Ballroom Dancing – well, why wouldn't it be so? I was a little girl, after all, and the thought of twirling around in all those beautiful gowns was so exciting that I wanted to join in. However, it turned out to be far more practical than that, I'm afraid, because the wonderful dresses only came after the achievement of a certain standard in dance. The dress for Ballroom Dancing actually should be, in the first place, both comfortable and appropriate to the particular style of dance; unrestricted freedom of movement must also be a consideration because it is important that you are able to move your arms, hips and legs freely.

Now, shoes! Well, as stated earlier, one should always buy good shoes, and this is especially so when wearing them for dancing, because those shoes must support and help you to do things with your feet that you wouldn't do generally when walking down the street. It is essential that shoes for Ballroom Dancing be lightweight, with a flexible sole, and if possible with a leather sole. Good dancers go one step further by wearing shoes with non-skid soles made of chrome leather or similar. For the woman, the shoes must have a heel – but not stiletto – for heels help the balance on backward steps, of which the woman has considerably more than the man. For men the rule is good-quality dress shoes.

You may now have embarked on a pastime that will 'dance' with you on your way through life. There again, you may have embarked on a pastime that will make you into a world champion. But whatever, everything is in now in place and you are dancing; job done and over, or is it just beginning? Who knows? Only time will tell.

After the Dance

This is the interesting part! If you are good, then after the dance everyone will want to be your partner. If you are, well, shall we say not quite so good, then what do you do? If you love dancing and have the *enthusiasm* as mentioned earlier on then you will go out, have more lessons and practise, practise, practise! And here is the more interesting part – if you are actually one of the good ones, then you too should go right out there and get yourself some more lessons and practise, practise, practise, for you may just go on and become a world champion – well, who knows?

After the World Championships then you can then pass on your knowledge and expertise to the up and coming generations; it is incredible just how many former world champions now have their own dance schools where they train and coach the new generation to climb the mountains they themselves conquered; it's a bit like a never-ending circle.

So, to sum up the answer to the earlier question, 'What is Ballroom Dancing?' The answer is, quite simply, 'Ballroom Dancing is social dancing.' It is given the term social dancing in that it requires social and physical contact, plus some form of interaction between those dancing together. In fact, even if you're not that good at it, there is a lot of fun to be had in such a pastime! Unlike some other forms of dance, the very young and the – dare I say it? – very old can participate. I mean, when did you last see a 90 year old on pointe? Never, I suspect, because it is neither sensible nor attractive! But to see your gran Waltz around the room at the age of 90 is sensible because she is getting gentle and healthy exercise whilst at the same time enjoying herself. And is it attractive? No, it is more than that: it is pure magic!

Ballroom Dancing is devoid of all the no-entry signs. It is a sport for anyone and everyone to enjoy, and on what level is entirely up to you; from amateur to professional, from enjoyment to championship level – the choice is yours. Whether you choose Ballroom Dancing or Latin American Dancing, the experience will be wonderful, for it is without doubt an exhilarating art form with a truly international following and appreciation. Young and old can 'do it', rich and poor, believers in God, believers in the universe; tall, small, fat and thin – all can take part and enjoy Ballroom Dancing

So come on, let's dance!

It's elegant, it's beautiful, it's charming – it's Ballroom Dancing, as demonstrated here by the great Frank & Peggy Spencer MBE. (Reproduced with kind permission of Peggy Spencer)

Chapter 3

GREAT NAMES IN THE WORLD OF BALLROOM DANCING

In each of my books I have chosen just a few people who can be deemed greats in their particular field. Of course, those chosen are of my own personal choices, but I do hope that if not all readers agree with me then a sizable proportion will do so. The criteria for making my choices remain fairly constant throughout this series of books, and that criteria is that each choice must have stood the test of time, and similarly each choice must be a name that is familiar to the man in the street and not just to those interested in the subject matter in hand.

In the world of Ballroom Dancing the measurement of achievement for individuals or experts is more straightforward and a little easier than it is in the other books in this series, for here in Ballroom Dancing there is in place an examination structure to assess the progress and standard of the dancers; there are also competitions where couples can prove that they are better than their contemporaries – on that particular day, anyway! But this isn't enough, for the man in the street would neither know, nor would he care, whether a dancer had a medal or had won a World Championship. Joe Public only affords recognition to those who entertain in the broader sense of the word – that is, through the medium of television, public demonstrations or stage shows, rather than by the great heights achieved on a personal level. It is, also, to these chosen and inspirational individuals that all dancers, young and old, amateur and professional, look for *their* inspiration, and so it is these individuals, the ones who also entertain Joe Public, who will then in turn appear in this section of the book to once more entertain and inform, only this time through the written word.

The chosen greats here then are – though not exclusively the only greats in this world of Ballroom Dancing, I hasten to add – Victor Silvester, Fred Astaire and Ginger Rogers, Frank and Peggy Spencer, Bill and Bobbie

Irvine, and more recently Len Goodman, each chosen for a specific reason. Victor Silvester is generally known as the daddy of Ballroom Dancing as we know it today, and so as a 'parent' then he most certainly deserves his place in this section! Fred Astaire and Ginger Rogers not only brought the joys of Ballroom Dancing to the silver screen, but through dance they enabled the world to dream and to escape the trials, tribulations and horrors of the turbulent times in which they lived. Frank and Peggy Spencer gave us the perfection and visually exciting dance form of Formation Dancing, thus opening up an entire new world for those who excelled at dance and yet lacked the confidence to dance in a pairs partnership; this in itself is inspirational in that it showed many that team work could be both rewarding and character building. Bill and Bobbie Irvine became one of the first in a stream of famous dancing pairs, thus inspiring many more greats who were to follow them. Finally last, but certainly not least, the silver-tongued and quick-witted 'man's man', and 'ladies man' for that matter, Len Goodman, who has spent a lifetime both dancing and judging dance and who in turn has become a modern-day hero for today's generation, showing them that dance is not only a life choice but can be a career choice too. He has taken the 'airy fairy' feel out of dance, which many would say it still carries, and brought dance to the man in the street as a great pastime for everyone.

So on that note, let me introduce you first to the man who it is only right to describe as the foundation upon which Modern Ballroom Dancing stands: Mr Victor Silvester OBE.

VICTOR SILVESTER OBE

Innovator, demonstrator and teacher of dance, musician and dance band leader

VICTOR SILVESTER'S CONTRIBUTION TO THE WORLD OF BALLROOM DANCING

- Victor Silvester was in the front line of the development of Ballroom Dancing and of the music to accompany this form of dance; music which he created with his internationally famous Victor Silvester Orchestra
- It was in 1922 that Victor Silvester, together with his partner Phyllis Clarke, won the very first World Standard Ballroom Dancing Championship

VICTOR SILVESTER: The Man and His Life

- Victor Marlborough Silvester was born on 25 February 1900 in Wembley, Middlesex as the second son of a vicar
- He was educated at Ardingly College, St John's School, Leatherhead and John Lyon School, Harrow, an education which was interrupted by the outbreak of the First World War
- Before he was even 15 years of age – 14 years and nine months to be precise – and during the First World War he ran away to join the British Army and was soon fighting on the Western Front
- He was horrified to find, though, that when in the army he was forced to take an active part in a firing squad, where 'victims' were executed for cowardice. Shell shock and trauma were not recognised in those days, and were sadly conditions from which many of those executed were suffering
- Victor's parents suspected that he had run away to join the army, but it was several years before he was found and they were proved to be right
- After the War had ended Victor began his studies and went up to Worcester College, Oxford. He later studied music at Trinity College, London
- In 1922 Victor Silvester won the first World Standard Ballroom Dancing Championship with Phyllis Clarke as his partner. In the same year he married Dorothy Newton, with whom he went on to have one son, Victor Silvester Jr.
- Between the First and Second World Wars Victor, and his wife Dorothy, opened their own dancing school
- In 1928 his book *Modern Ballroom Dancing* was published and was an immediate bestseller, and is in fact still in print at the time of going to press
- He was a founder member of the Ballroom Committee of the Imperial Society of Teachers of Dancing (ISTD), which codified the theory and practice of Ballroom Dancing; and he later became President of the ISTD
- It was the lack of suitable music for dancing that prompted Victor Silvester in 1935 to form his own orchestra, which continued performing until the 1990s, with Victor Silvester Jr taking over from his father in 1971
- His first record was called 'You're Dancing on My Heart' and became the signature tune for his orchestra

- During the Second World War years Victor gave dancing lessons on the radio as a part of a radio programme called *The BBC Dancing Club*, which was broadcast by the BBC
- In 1948, three years after the War had ended, *The BBC Dancing Club* was transferred from radio to television, where it continued broadcasting for over 17 years
- 1958 saw the publication of his autobiography, *Dancing is My Life*
- In 1961 Victor Silvester was awarded an OBE for services to Ballroom Dancing
- He retired in 1971
- In 1972, in recognition of his charity work, Victor Silvester was appointed President of the Lord's Taverners
- Victor Silvester died on holiday in Aiguebelle on the Côte d' Azur, France, while he was swimming in the sea. The date was 14 August 1978
- After his death, his world famous orchestra lived on, presided over by Victor Silvester Jr, until he too died in 1991

AND FINALLY …

- He sold more than 75 million copies of the recordings he made with his orchestra, thus becoming one of the biggest selling recording artists of all time
- Nelson Mandela mentioned Victor Silvester's music as an inspiration during his time of incarceration

And so we now move on to the next great. However, this time it is not one great but a pair in the form of Fred Astaire and Ginger Rogers, affectionately known the world over as Fred and Ginger – or even as Fred and Ginge come to that. It was this remarkable pair that brought the world of escapism to the silver screen, at a time when all seemed to be doom and gloom.

FRED ASTAIRE AND GINGER ROGERS

Dancers of the silver screen

It is so easy to think of these two as one, but in fact they were both masters in their own right. However, when they came together they created a magic never before seen and, some say, never seen since. They may have been two individuals, but they danced as one.

FRED ASTAIRE'S CONTRIBUTION TO THE WORLD OF BALLROOM DANCING

Probably his most outstanding contribution to the world of dance was his ability to create the most innovative of dance moves.

FRED ASTAIRE: The Man and His Life

- Fred Astaire was born on 10 May 1899 in Omaha, Nebraska as Frederick Austerlitz, the son of Frederic E Austerlitz and Ann Geilus Austerlitz
- He attended his first Ballet class at the age of four and soon after studied Tap Dancing with Ned Wayburn, who was one of the pioneers of Modern Tap Dancing
- He soon became a 'performing child' as one half of a duo with his sister, Adele, who was just eighteen months older than him
- The Austerlitzes decided to change their surname to Astaire with the advent of the First World War
- Astaire's 'career' as a child performer with his sister Adele meant in fact that he had little formal schooling and so was in general taught by his mother
- When they reached their teens the brother and sister soon began to make their new name famous in the world of dance; a name that was later to become synonymous with the word 'dance'
- Fred and Adele Astaire made their Broadway debut in 1917 in a musical revue called *Over the Top*
- The Astaires danced their way through various successes in the 1920s until Adele retired from showbusiness in order to marry Lord Charles Cavendish
- This was initially a worrying time for Fred, as Adele was generally considered the better dancer of the pair but, despite not being conventional leading-man material, Fred Astaire went on to establish himself as great performer
- After his sister's retirement Fred teamed up for a time with Claire Luce
- Things were all set to change though, for up until this point Fred had been a stage performer and then in 1933 he teamed up with Ginger

Rogers in a partnership that was to become a phenomenon, known the world over as Fred and Ginger

- In the same year he married Phyllis Livingston Potter with whom he had two children, a son, Fred Jr (born in 1936), and a daughter, Ava (born in 1942). Phyllis also had a son, Peter, from a previous marriage
- In 1946 Fred Astaire announced his decision to retire, and he did, but it was a retirement that was to last for less than two years
- In 1948 he came to the rescue when Gene Kelly injured himself whilst rehearsing for the film *Easter Parade* and Astaire stepped in to help, thus ending his short-lived retirement
- In 1955 Phyllis died of cancer
- In 1980, when he was 81 years old, Astaire married his second wife, Robyn Smith, who was then only 35 years old and a former jockey
- Fred Astaire died of pneumonia in Los Angeles, California on 22 June 1987. He was 88 years old

AND FINALLY …

- He was known for his laid-back and relaxed style, yet he was actually a workaholic and a perfectionist
- Fred Astaire continued to dance until he was in his 70s and only gave up when he felt that his age, and so his agility, was stopping him from performing at the level at which he wanted. He continued with his film career, however, until he was in his 80s
- He was an avid horse racing fan, a passion he shared with his second wife, Robyn

GINGER ROGERS' CONTRIBUTION TO THE WORLD OF BALLROOM DANCING

Ginger Rogers brought her wealth of versatility to the world of Ballroom Dancing, as well as an ease and gracefulness in performance that has never been forgotten.

GINGER ROGERS: The Woman and Her Life

- Ginger Rogers was born Virginia Katherine McMath on 16 July 1911 in Independence, Missouri as the only child of William Eddins McMath and Lela Emogene (Owens)

- Her parents separated before her birth and her mother later went on to marry her second husband, John Rogers, whom Ginger treated as her father
- She was, as they say, born to dance and by the age of 10 was appearing in charity shows under the name of Ginger Rogers – Rogers being her stepfather's name
- By the age of 14 she was a professional touring artiste and was soon both a hit on stage and screen, and had in fact made 19 films before teaming up with Fred Astaire on the film *Flying Down to Rio*
- In 1929 Ginger made her Broadway debut in *Top Speed*
- The following year she starred in *Girl Crazy* on Broadway
- In 1931 Ginger Rogers appeared in *Tip Off*, her first Hollywood film
- Ginger won an Oscar in 1940 for Best Actress in the leading role of *Kitty Foyle*
- Ginger Rogers was a woman of many talents. She was an accomplished artist, being both a painter and a sculptress; she was also an outstanding athlete, excelling in many areas and the winner of many tennis cups; she also designed a lingerie line
- It seems that Ginger's talents were limitless, for not only did she appear in shows, but she directed too, and in fact directed her first stage musical at the age of 74
- She was married five times, with the first time being in 1931 and the last in 1961. All her marriages, however, ended in divorce. The one famously enduring relationship in her life was with her mother, to whom she was devoted
- Ginger Rogers died of natural causes on 25 April 1995 in Rancho Mirage, California USA
- Ginger Rogers and her mother are buried side by side, with the grave of Fred Astaire just yards away

AND FINALLY …

- The name Ginger allegedly came about when her little cousin couldn't pronounce Virginia correctly

What makes Fred and Ginger so special is that they weren't 'just' dancers, but artists in every sense of the word, and this brought a greater artistic depth to their performances. As well as their musical films, they also had a string of other films and stage performances to their names, including:

Musical Films Featuring Fred Astaire and Ginger Rogers Together Include:

Barkleys of Broadway (The)
Carefree
Flying Down to Rio
Follow the Fleet
Gay Divorcee (The)
Roberta
Shall We Dance
Story of Vernon and Irene Castle (The)
Swing Time
Top Hat

Musical Films Featuring Fred Astaire Include:

Band Wagon (The)
Belle of New York (The)
Blue Skies
Broadway Melody
Broadway Melody of 1940
Daddy Long Legs
Damsel in Distress (A)
Dancing Lady
Easter Parade
Finian's Rainbow
Funny Face
Holiday Inn
Let's Dance
Royal Wedding
Second Chorus
Silk Stockings
That's Entertainment
Three Little Words
Yolanda and the Thief

You Were Never Lovelier
You'll Never Get Rich
Ziegfield Follies

Non-Musical Films Featuring Fred Astaire Include:
Amazing Dobermans (The)
Ghost Story
Midas Run (The)
Notorious Landlady (The)
On the Beach
Pleasure of His Company (The)
Purple Taxi (The)
Sky's the Limit (The)
Towering Inferno (The)

Non-Musical Films Featuring Ginger Rogers Include:
Bachelor Mother
The Barkleys of Broadway
Black Widow
Carefree
Confession
Dreamboat
Fifth Avenue Girl
First Traveling Saleslady (The)
Forever Female
Groom Wore Spurs (The)
Harlow (The)
Having Wonderful Time
Heartbeat
I'll Be Seeing You
It Had to Be You
Kitty Foyle
Lady in the Dark
Lucky Partners
Magnificent Doll
Major and the Minor (The)

Monkey Business
Oh! Men, Oh! Women
Once Upon a Honeymoon
Perfect Strangers
Primrose Path
Roxie Hart
Storm Warning
Tales of Manhattan
Teenage Rebel
Tender Comrade
Tight Spot
Tom, Dick and Harry
Twist of Fate
Vivacious Lady
Weekend at the Waldorf
We're Not Married

Stage Appearances of Ginger Rogers Include:
40 Carats
Annie Get Your Gun
Anything Goes
Bell, Book and Candle
Calamity Jane
Charley's Aunt
Coco
Ginger Rogers Show (The)
Girl Crazy
Hello, Dolly!
Husband and Wife
Love and Let Love
Mame
Miss Moffat
More Perfect Union (The)
No, No, Nanette
Pink Jungle (The)
Top Speed

Tovarich
Unsinkable Molly Brown (The)
Vaudeville Theatres

So we move on now to another pair of dancers, but this time it is not for their own dancing abilities that they won international acclaim, nor even for training other pairs. This time it was for training entire teams of dancers, who went on to astound and amaze us all with their faultless precision. All of these dancers were of course trained by the formidable Frank and Peggy Spencer MBE.

FRANK AND PEGGY SPENCER MBE

A pair of dancers who epitomise the elegance and sophistication of Ballroom Dancing

FRANK AND PEGGY SPENCER'S CONTRIBUTION TO THE WORLD OF DANCE

Together they gave dancers the greatest gift of all; they gave them the courage and belief in themselves and the ability to succeed as a part of a team, when feeling as individuals that they would never shine.

The names of Frank and Peggy Spencer are synonymous with the words Formation Dancing. Dancing in time with your partner is a wonderful feat indeed, but just imagine up to eight couples not only dancing in time with each other, but dancing in time with the other seven couples on the floor too. Add to that the complication of different rhythms with all the dancing partners forming the most intricate dance patterns across the floor too, and you have the magic that is Formation Dancing.

It was Frank and Peggy Spencer who were, for 50 years, considered to be the masters of the art of Formation Dancing. Sadly, though, this form of dance is not as popular now as it was in the Spencer years, and to be honest I feel sure that this is because, in the UK anyway, it is a ship without a captain. (There are, though, I hasten to add, many Formation dance teams throughout Europe and the USA.) However, it would be difficult to find anyone to equal the talent and expertise Frank and Peggy brought to the planning and choreography of their many championship teams and so it is that at this moment in time this ship is floundering at sea. On a more optimistic note, there are new teams forming in the universities of the UK, and so one can only hope that some equally talented younger blood will come along and take the helm to help steer the luxury liner back on its course once more.

So who were these two remarkable people and exactly what kind of people were they? Well, the first answer that springs to mind is 'private', for information on them is very thin on the ground – and in the case of Frank Spencer it is almost non-existent – and so where their achievements warrant an extensive biography, information on the Spencers themselves, I am sad to say, is short but sweet.

PEGGY SPENCER: The Woman and Her Life

- Peggy Spencer was born as Margaret Ann Hull on 24 September 1920 to an Irish mother (Maggie) and English father (Jim)
- Her mother was a feisty woman, born in Dublin during the uprising
- Her father was a London-born Cockney who soon changed Margaret Ann's name to 'Peggy'
- It was a happy childhood for Peggy, who was born and brought up in Bromley, Kent, with her two brothers and a sister
- In her teens Peggy became more interested in politics than in dancing and was in fact all set to follow a career in that direction until the advent of the Second World War changed things
- Peggy married Jack Spencer in 1940 and together they went on to have two children, Helena and Michael; Peggy and Jack, however, divorced in 1947
- It was during the war years that Peggy's love of dancing began in earnest when, together with her sister-in law, she started teaching dance to beginners in Sydenham, in between the air raids
- In the year 2004 Peggy Spencer became President of the Imperial Society of Teachers of Dancing
- She 'retired' to King's Lynn in Norfolk in order to be closer to her daughter, Helena
- Within four years of her retirement she was invited to be Lady Mayoress of King's Lynn

- At the time of going to press the wonderfully talented, enthusiastic and exuberant Peggy Spencer was still teaching beginners and intermediate dancers as well as sharing her experiences with various organisations through a series of talk given to the lucky residents of Norfolk – how pleased they must be that this wonderful national treasure chose dance over politics, but it does make one wonder what could have been for us all had she chosen politics. I doubt that anyone would have dared put a foot out of line had that been the case!

FRANK SPENCER: The Man and His Life

- Frank Spencer was born in October 1903 in south-east London as one in a family of five children
- A talented sportsman, he played cricket for Beckenham
- As he grew up he also became very interested in music and dancing
- His first dance partner was Doris Nichols of Beckenham and it was with her that he went on to the finals of the World Championships in Paris

FRANK AND PEGGY SPENCER AS A PROFESSIONAL DANCE PARTNERSHIP

- The war had ended, and so too had not only Peggy's marriage to Jack Spencer but Frank's marriage too – Frank was actually Peggy's brother-in-law
- It was then that Frank and Peggy went on to form one of the most successful and enduring dancing partnerships of all time
- In the 1960s this professional partnership then became a romantic partnership with their marriage to each other
- They then went on to set up their own dance school in Penge, south London, called the Royston Ballroom. It was here that their Formation days began and where they formed and trained the Frank and Peggy Spencer Penge Formation Dancing Team
- For almost 50 years Frank and Peggy Spencer's Formation Dancing teams appeared in the TV programme *Come Dancing*
- During their professional work Frank and Peggy travelled the world, teaching, adjudicating and promoting British Ballroom and Latin American Dancing, and for this lifetime's work they each received the MBE during the Queen's Jubilee year in 1977

- They were also honoured with no fewer than eight Carl Alan Awards
- Twice they were invited to dance at Buckingham Palace and they appeared in the Royal Command Performance on more than one occasion too
- Their popularity with the Royals also extended beyond the shores of Britain, with the Spencers being invited by the Monaco Royal Family to teach Prince Albert and Princess Stephanie to dance in preparation for their 'coming out' balls
- After Frank's death, Peggy continued with her dancing school in Penge, together with her business partner, Geoffrey Hearne

Peggy Spencer – Formation Dance Royalty meets Prince Rainier. (Reproduced with kind permission of Peggy Spencer)

THE FRANK AND PEGGY SPENCER FORMATION DANCE TEAMS

During their years as dance teachers Frank and Peggy came to realise that there were many young dancers in their schools who would never have the confidence to shine as individuals but who, given the opportunity, might shine as part of a group. And so the seed of the Frank and Peggy Spencer Formation Dance Teams had been sown.

Frank and Peggy then put together their first teams of couples, matching them against each other in competitions; they explored the idea of different dances, which were then choreographed to make up a group routine. They started first by using the Waltz, but then added other dances with each segueing effortlessly into the next, the final outcome of which was the birth of Formation Dancing.

What some are inclined to forget is that Formation Dancing is as difficult as single or paired dancing, requiring not only personal dedication to learn the complex routines but also the co-operation to learn the complex routines in exactly the same manner as the other couples in the formation, with no room for personal nuances. As with all sport, the dancers had to be in the peak of condition and so exercise regimes were soon put in place to ensure the health and fitness of all team members; any weakness in any team member would inevitably reflect on the performance of the team as a whole, which was totally unacceptable to the perfectionist Spencers.

Theatre is a visual art and as dance is an arm of the theatrical experience then what we see must extend beyond technique. In the early days Peggy appreciated and embraced this by designing the costumes herself. This made complete sense as she, more than anyone else, in this new form of dance knew the feel and artistic flow of a formation piece and so was able to design the dresses both to enhance and progress the piece in the correct visual direction. Initially the dresses were made by the parents and friends of the dancers, though once the teams were featured on the television then that all had to change, and the dresses had to be made by professional dressmakers.

Formation Dancing became a hugely successful form of dancing, though always was, and is in fact to this day, an amateur form of dance. Now, whether this is a good or bad thing is certainly not for me to say, but it does occur to me that it must have been, and again still must be, very difficult for teams of Formation Dancers and their trainers to reach the standards set by Frank and Peggy when they have to devote huge chunks of their lives to earning a living and maybe even raising a family. And for that reason – if no other – one has to stand back in awe and wonder.

When Frank was no longer able to help with the teams, Peggy continued to train no fewer than 21 championship teams with her business partner, Geoffrey Hearn. The word 'retirement' is clearly not in Peggy's dictionary, a fact brought home to me when she, an incredibly busy lady, generously agreed to talk to me about her formation career; surely a lady of her grand age would have a lot of spare time, and so it wouldn't be too much of a hassle for her. Right? Wrong! This lady it would seem is forever on the go, because she is as passionate now as she was ever about her art.

The great Peggy Spencer celebrates her 88th birthday with all the grace and charm for which she is renowned. (Reproduced with kind permission of Peggy Spencer)

The world of dance owes a great deal to this beautiful, gracious and kind individual who, when she was training formation teams, was frequently invited to travel abroad to help other teachers set up their own teams and who today, as she dances on into her ninth decade, continues to give generously to the world of dance. Formation Dancing may be the amateur aim of Ballroom Dancing but Peggy Spencer MBE certainly is not. She has worked, lived and danced her dream – a dance that is a never-ending lifetime of dreams; it is she who in the year 2010 will be 90 years old and is she who is *The Professional Lady* of Ballroom Dancing.

We now move on from one elegant and sophisticated pair to another, Bill and Bobbie Irvine MBE. This charismatic pair has inspired hundreds of budding champions to follow their dream – or maybe it would be more accurate to say thousands! The image of Bobbie Irvine forever etched on my mind is of a lady with a silver flash in her hair and a small dog tucked under her arm.

BILL AND BOBBIE IRVINE MBE

A charismatic pair and winners of thirteen world titles

BILL (WILLIAM) IRVINE: The Man and His Life

- Bill was born in Kilsyth, Scotland, where there is now even a street name after him
- He was from a mining family and unusually took up dancing relatively late in life – after he had completed his military service – and it wasn't in fact until he was 22 years old that he had his first dancing lesson
- He was a butcher's assistant before he became a dancer, though he did used to practise his dancing behind the butcher's horse and cart when he was supposed to be out simply making deliveries. I'm not sure how that would go down today – and I'm not talking about the horse & cart either!
- In 1948 Bill took and passed his first Associate examination
- He spent some time in South Africa as a young man after he accepted an invitation to work for John Wells and Renee Sissons, former champions, in their school in Johannesburg. It was whilst there that he met his future wife and dance partner, Bobbie Barwell

- Bill and Bobbie married in 1957 and went on to become South African Ballroom Champions before settling in England
- As well as a performer Bill Irvine was also a teacher and world-class adjudicator
- He, quite unusually, never competed as an amateur dancer, but only as a professional
- During his lifetime he also became known for his work in senior administrative roles in dancing, becoming Chairman of the Modern Ballroom Faculty of the ISTD and later becoming Vice President and then President of the Society

BOBBIE IRVINE: The Woman and Her Life

- Bobbie Irvine was born Bobbie Barwell in Oudshoorn, South Africa
- Her father was an executive with Shell
- Her parents expected to have a boy, whom they intended to name Robert and so when a girl arrived, not liking the name Roberta, they decided to call her Bobbie
- She began dancing classes early on in her life and made her first stage appearance at the age of three
- In a desperate attempt to curb her passion for dancing and encourage her to study, her father sent her to be educated at a strict convent school but – thankfully, for the world of Ballroom Dancing and of course the rest of us mere mortals too – his attempt failed!
- Before becoming a professional dancer, Bobbie spent a short spell as a model
- Her love of dancing never left her and even later in life she never really retired from dancing, even teaching during her battle with cancer

BILL AND BOBBIE IRVINE AS A PROFESSIONAL DANCE PARTNERSHIP

- When the pair first met each had other dance partners; Bill's partner was Aida Kruger and Bobbie's partner was Vernon Ballantyne
- In 1955 Bobbie and Vernon Ballantyne beat Bill and Aida Kruger in the South African Championships. Both couples were then selected to compete in London against Britain and Australia. However, both couples were subsequently defeated and it was at this point that Ballroom history

was about to be made, for it was then that both Kruger and Ballantyne decided to retire with the outcome being that Bill and Bobbie got together to form one of the greatest and longest-lasting dance partnerships of all time

- Bill Irvine married Bobbie Barwell in1957
- In 1960 Bill and Bobbie Irvine won their first World Ballroom Championships title in Berlin
- 1962 saw the pair win their first British Championship
- In 1967 they were awarded the MBE for services to dance – the first time Ballroom Dancing had been recognised in the Queen's Honours List
- It was in 1968 that this now formidable pair achieved a remarkable feat unequalled before this date and – at the time of going to press – since when they won both the Standard and Latin American World Championships, on the same day!
- As well as a performer Bobbie Irvine was also a teacher and, as was Bill, a world-class adjudicator
- She was what can only be described as an 'elegant and glamorous character' known for the trademark white streak in her dark hair and for her love of good chocolate and small dogs
- Bobbie died in 2004 and Bill in 2008
- During their outstanding dance career Bill and Bobbie Irvine won thirteen world titles

BILL AND BOBBIE IRVINE: PRINCIPAL PROFESSIONAL CHAMPIONSHIPS

1960   World 9 Dance, World Ballroom
1961   World Latin
1962   World 9 Dance International, British and World Ballroom
1963   World, British Star and International Ballroom, World 9 Dance
1964   World, British and Star Ballroom
1965   World and Star Latin
1966   World, British and Star Ballroom
1967   World and Star Ballroom
1968   Star Ballroom, World Ballroom, World Latin

(The information above is taken from Bill and Bobbie Irvine's book *The Dancing Years*.)

So from one dancing pair we move on to just one 'youngster' – amazing how comparisons can knock off years, isn't it! Alright, so Len Goodman might not be in his twenties, but he has a boyish charm that has brought Ballroom Dancing to the masses and made him loved by a nation as they sit glued to the TV for the annual broadcasting of *Strictly Come Dancing*. Len Goodman has made an extraordinary sport appear ordinary and accessible, and that in itself is a great achievement.

LEN GOODMAN

Silver-tongued professional dance adjudicator, teacher and dancer

LEN GOODMANS CONTRIBUTION TO THE WORLD OF BALLROOM DANCING

His cheeky-chappie approach to dancing, and to life in general, gives to Ballroom a credibility with the man in the street that some of the other forms of dance clearly lack.

LEN GOODMAN: The Man and His Life

- Len Goodman was born Leonard Gordon Goodman in Farnborough, Kent in 1944 as the son of Leonard Gordon and Louisa Adelaide (née Eldridge) Goodman
- His father was an electrician and the family lived with his maternal grandparents; his barrow boy grandfather was a great influence on him as a child
- His grandfather progressed from selling wares from a market stall on to owning two shops on Bethnal Green Road
- In about 1950 the Goodman family moved to Blackfen in Kent where his parents bought a greengrocer's shop
- In the mid 1950s his parents separated, eventually both finding happiness with other partners
- Not academically gifted, Len left school at 15 years old and went to work as a dockyard welder on the ships
- When he was around 20 years old he broke his foot playing five-a-side football after work, and ironically it was Ballroom Dancing that the doctor suggested as a form of rehabilitation

- Len was then spotted at the local dance school by former world champion dancer and top coach Henry Kingston, who then asked him to partner his daughter Cherry and to train for competitions. The Ballroom career of Len Goodman had finally started, much later than is 'normal' in this world
- On 27 April 1972 Len Goodman married his dancing partner, Cherry Kingston, but they later divorced when Cheryl left him for a Frenchman
- Following another relationship Len's son, James William Goodman, was born in 1981
- Having retired from competitive dancing Len had by now a thriving dance school in Dartford, Kent and was recognised as an international dance competition judge and lecturer
- 38 years later and at the time of going to press, the dance school is still going strong and thousands have learnt to dance various dance styles thanks to Len's fun way of teaching
- In the year 1993 Len's father died followed by his mother four years later
- Len Goodman was invited to join the judging panel of the successful TV show *Strictly Come Dancing* when it was launched in 2004. The rest, as they say, is history

AND FINALLY …

- Len Goodman is famous for the saucy sayings which he gives out as the Head Judge on BBC TV's *Strictly* programme, sayings such as: 'Lovely rise and fall, up and down like a bride's nightie.' 'You're just like a trifle, fruity up the top but a little bit spongy down below,' and the most celebrated of all his sayings, the one for which he has become famous is, 'All sizzle, no sausage,' which apparently means all flash and no substance
- Len is also a judge on the American version of *Strictly*, though there it is called *Dancing with the Stars*

We now move on to some of those other names who make this world so exciting and so glamorous. They are the ones who not only made it what it was yesterday, but who make it what it is today and what, by their example, it will go on to be for time immemorial. *They* are our inspiration to dance.

Chapter 4

WHO'S WHO IN THE WORLD OF BALLROOM DANCING

A ll professions have their supporting pillars, and by that I mean the experts who hold up that particular house of knowledge. It might be the Medical House, where the pillars include world-class surgeons or the research scientists in pursuit of cures for illnesses that plague mankind; it might be the Legal House, where lawyers uphold the

Alan and Hazel Fletcher.
(Reproduced with kind
permission of Alan and
Hazel Fletcher)

laws to keep us all safe, or the House of Education, where professors of various disciplines teach the teachers exactly how to teach us. On and on it goes, for it is the way of the world, and so it figures that the Ballroom House will have its supporting pillars too, those who have passed on their expertise or those who will; those who have kept this house in order for the rest of us to enjoy. Below you will find a selection – not all, I hasten to add – of Ballroom pillars for you to browse over and perhaps, as a result, aspire to one day join. Sadly, for some notable contributors to this very special world of Ballroom Dancing, the information was not readily available, despite hours of research, and so there are some who should rightly have been included but I have had no choice but to omit. So to begin we will take a look at the legendary Alan and Hazel Fletcher, whose love and enthusiasm exude from every bone in their dancing bodies, as I discovered during a lengthy phone call with Hazel. I think there is nothing as wonderfully infectious as an expert who is passionate about his or her art and career, for it is then that others are inspired to tread in his or her footsteps to glory.

ALAN AND HAZEL FLETCHER

Speciality: Latin American

ALAN FLETCHER: The Man and His Life

- Alan Fletcher was born in 1947 as the second son of Ernest and Violet Fletcher
- His father, Ernest, was a St John Ambulance driver before becoming a general foreman on large building projects and then finally a chief baggage handler with British Airways. His mother, Violet, was a seamstress – all, it would seem, a million miles away from the life that awaited Alan
- Alan was educated at Langley Secondary Modern School in Langley, Buckinghamshire
- As a youngster he was initially a keen footballer, until a friend that is persuaded him that dancing was fun too. In no time at all Alan was hooked and on his way, his only sadness being that with the advent of dancing he had to end his Saturday afternoons playing football!
- He was only nine years old when he discovered the joys of dance, and this was at a time when dancing for boys was not as acceptable as it is today

Nevertheless, he was soon a juvenile and then junior finalist in all the major Ballroom and Latin American events

- Not only did Alan enjoy, and excel, at both Ballroom and Latin American dance but he also became a member of the highly successful Slough Junior Formation Team, trained by Ken Bateman and Blanche Ingle, competing and travelling throughout Europe
- Alan was soon competing in Formation and open competitions in Ballroom and Latin American at the same time until the pressure caused by the shortage of practice forced him to take the decision to specialise in open competitions only. He did not return to Formation Dance for many years, and even then it was as a trainer rather than as a competitor
- It was in the year 1965 that the now famous Alan and Hazel Fletcher dance partnership began – and it was almost by accident! Alan and Hazel were in fact boyfriend and girlfriend when he was looking for a new dance partner, never realising she was right under his nose all the time
- Alan was an experienced dancer and Hazel a mere beginner in Ballroom and Latin American. She did have twelve years' Ballet experience, but did not seem to be a likely candidate as a possible future partner. Fortunately for the dance world though, Alan's dance teacher had other ideas, and so brought the pair together, with the result being that Hazel became Alan's new official dance partner
- In 1968 Alan and Hazel married, becoming the famous Fletcher partnership in more ways than one
- After dancing together for four years the Fletchers realised their first ambition when they were selected for the British Team
- Success was then never far away, including the World Amateur Latin American Championships which they won in both 1972 and 1973
- In December 1973, after the 2nd World title win, they hung up their amateur shoes and turned professional
- Life then became such a hectic round of demonstrations, competitions and teaching that they took their decision one step farther and turned full time professionals within the first 6 months of their Professional career
- From then on, until their retirement from competitive dancing in 1981, Alan and Hazel won all the major championships, during which time they were undefeated in Latin American both in the World Championships (1977–1981) and the European Championships (1976–1980)

- And so it was that after the World Championships in May 1981, they decided the time had come for them to retire from the competitive scene. Their farewell performance was at the British Team Match in Blackpool, where a lengthy standing ovation was their reward
- Towards the end of their competitive career Alan and Hazel took on the role of becoming Formation Dance trainers and achieved tremendous success with two German Formation Dance teams which, under their tutorship became World and European Champions
- In 1985 Alan and Hazel, together with the Norwegian champions Espen and Kirsten Salberg, devised the cabaret show '*Latin Fantasy*', followed by two further cabaret shows over the next seven years.
- However, retiring from the world of dance completely was never on the agenda and so they continue, to this day, to share their knowledge and expertise with aspiring dancers – on an international basis – being in demand throughout the world as teachers, lecturers and adjudicators.

HAZEL FLETCHER: The Woman and Her Life

- Hazel Fletcher was born in 1948 as the eldest of three children born to Leslie and Kathleen Simpson
- Leslie Simpson originally trained and worked as a carpenter, though went on to work as a quality controller for Mars Confectionary until his retirement; Kathleen worked as a secretary for many years and also as a dressmaker
- Hazel began dancing at the age of three and for 12 years studied Classical Ballet
- By the age of 14, Hazel realized that she would probably prefer to teach ballet rather than to perform it
- She was, in fact, 15 years old before the Latin American bug bit her when she watched her first competition. It was the partnership element of Latin that excited her, as well as the passion of the Latin American music. The desire to perform was thus re-kindled and this time burned more fiercely than before
- In 1965 Alan Fletcher was looking for a new dance partner when his teacher suggested that his own girlfriend, Hazel, could be the one to put an end to his search
- As a result of this teacher's foresight, the Alan and Hazel Fletcher dance partnership was formed

- In 1968 Hazel and Alan's partnership became formal in another way too – with their marriage
- Dancing as amateurs, the Fletchers won the World Amateur Latin American Championships both in 1972 and 1973, after which they turned professional
- They then went on to repeat their amateur successes on the professional circuit until in May 1981 Hazel and Alan ended their professional, competing career on a high when, as five times undefeated World and European Champions, they retired from the competitive circuit.
- 1985 saw a diversification in their talents when, together with Espen and Kirsten Salberg (Norwegian championship dancers and runners up to Alan and Hazel in their final years of competing), they produced the cabaret show, *"Latin Fantasy"*
- This Anglo/Norwegian partnership lasted a further seven years and resulted in another two shows
- Hazel, along with her husband, Alan, not only continues to teach, lecture and judge around the world but also finds the best in the world knocking at their door hoping to soak up their expertise and emulate their past successes
- It is doubtful that Hazel will ever fully retire from dance but she has at least now reached a time in her life when she can spend more time with, and enjoy, her Godchildren and dogs, whilst her husband now has time to drive more balls, more often, on the golf course and have more time for his great passion of football too, especially more time for his beloved Arsenal – having been a fan since he was a small child – maybe that nine year old boy has finally returned to follow his childhood passion!

ANTON DU BEKE AND ERIN BOAG

Speciality: Ballroom

ANTON DU BEKE: The Man and His Life

- Anton Du Beke was born on 20 July 1966
- He has a romantic heritage as well as a romantic sounding name, for his mother is Spanish and his father Hungarian, although Anton himself was born and raised in Sevenoaks, Kent, together with his brother and sister

- In the world of dance he was quite a late starter – 14 years old to be precise. Until that point in time he was actually more interested in football than he was in Ballroom Dancing; then he realised that girls in fact were more interested in Ballroom Dancing than they were in playing football, and so he switched allegiance
- At 5'11" tall he is the perfect height for the elegance of Ballroom Dancing and, although expert in both Latin American and Ballroom Dance, his heart is in and his passion is for Ballroom, for he loves the accompanying tradition and style of Ballroom Dancing
- Anton is also trained in Ballet, Contemporary, Jazz and Modern Theatre Dance
- He is a veteran TV celebrity and a gifted entertainer appearing on a wide variety of television shows, as well as making numerous stage appearances
- Most people say to anyone in the world of entertainment, 'Don't give up the day job!' Anton, however, didn't have a day job; he had a night job, getting up at 3.00am to work as a baker, thus freeing his afternoons to train as a dancer and they say it's a glamorous world!
- In 1997 Anton met his partner Erin Boag when she moved from Australia to England, and they soon became a competitive pair
- In 2002 Anton and Erin turned professional
- Anton Du Beke and Erin Boag were theatre choreographers for the hit, live show *Simply Ballroom* and made a special guest appearance in a gala performance at the Theatre Royal, Drury Lane in 2006
- *Simply Ballroom* has also been filmed for DVD by Universal Pictures
- In the year 2007 his book *Anton's Dance Class* was published by Kyle Cathie Ltd and is a hugely popular step by step guide to the major Ballroom and Latin American dances
- In 2009 Anton and Erin's show *Cheek to Cheek* toured the UK before coming into the West End
- In January 2010 Anton and Erin began a tour with their new show *Steppin' Out with Anton and Erin*
- Anton and Erin are also well known and popular professional dancers who have appeared on the TV show *Strictly Come Dancing*
- Like most other professionals, Anton Du Beke passes on his knowledge by teaching – when he can find the time of course!

ERIN BOAG: The Woman and Her Life

- Born on 17 March 1975, Erin originates from New Zealand where, as the daughter of professional dancers, she began her own dance training at the very young age of just three, learning Ballet, Tap, Jazz, Ballroom and Latin
- Not just a dancer, Erin is an all round sportswoman and is especially known as a top class swimmer
- When she was 15 years old, she travelled to Australia to watch a big competition. This, it turned out, was the defining moment in her life, the moment when she decided that she wanted to make dancing her career
- At the age of 18 she became New Zealand 10 Dance Amateur Champion
- When she was 19 years old she moved to Australia where she continued training, representing New Zealand in the 1995 and 1996 World Championships
- She then later moved to the UK to further her dance training
- It was in the UK in 1997 that she met Anton Du Beke, who was to become her long term dance partner
- In 1998 and 1999 Erin and her new partner, Anton, won the New Zealand Ballroom Championships as amateurs
- Together they both turned professional in 2002
- In 2004 Erin appeared in the Royal Variety performance
- The live show, *Simply Ballroom* was choreographed by Erin and Anton
- Erin, along with her partner Anton, hosted and danced in the Simply Ballroom DVD by Universal Pictures
- In 2007 Erin Boag and Karen Hardy worked together on the *Strictly Come Dancersize* DVD by 2Entertain, which they jointly choreographed and in which they both appeared
- Erin toured the UK with her partner, Anton Dn Beke, in their show *Cheek by Cheek* which also played the West End
- In 2009 Erin, along with Anton, coached and choreographed a group of South London teenagers for the Sky 1 reality show *Ballroom High*.
- 2010 saw another UK tour with Anton, this time called '*Steppin' Out with Anton and Erin*.'
- Some of the Ballroom dresses used in the stage shows, *Simply Ballroom*, *Cheek to Cheek* and *Steppin' Out*, have been designed by Erin – making Erin Boag '*an outstanding dancer*', '*an outstanding sportswoman*' and '*an outstanding designer*' – and so making one wonder, What next?

ARLENE PHILIPS OBE

The Woman and Her Life

- Arlene was born 22 May 1943 in Manchester, England, as one of three children
- When she was only 15 years old she lost her mother to leukaemia, an early tragedy in life the like from which, she readily admits, one never really recovers
- Encouraged by her mother, she started dance classes when she was just three years old and then later went on to full time training at the age of 16 years, at the Muriel Tweedy School in Manchester
- After completing her training in Manchester, and inspired by the work of Molly Molloy, Arlene moved to London to pursue a professional career in the world of dance
- Her first professional job was to choreograph a commercial for Lyons Maid Ice Cream, which featured a dancing milkmaid and a dancing cow; this was then followed by two Dr Pepper commercials
- When she was 27 Arlene married her first husband, 18 year old fashion designer Danny Noble; the marriage lasted seven years
- Arlene later appeared in the cast of *Flowers* on Broadway in 1974
- In 1974 she also created the famous and, at that time, innovative dance group Hot Gossip, becoming both its Director and Choreographer
- In 1978 *Hot Gossip* were invited to appear on the Kenny Everett TV show
- When she was 42 years old she married her second husband, a set designer called Angus Ion; he too was younger than Arlene – this time by 11 years; together Arlene and Angus went on to have their daughter, Abi, when Arlene was 47 years old; she already had another daughter, Alana, from an earlier relationship
- Her career then centered on choreographing pop videos for the likes of Duran Duran and the legendary Freddie Mercury; after Freddie's death she went on to choreograph the Queen musical, *We Will Rock You*, at the Dominion Theatre in London's West End
- Arlene Philips is known as a Jazz Dance choreographer and has choreographed numerous West End stage shows, such as *Starlight Express*, *Grease* and *Saturday Night Fever*
- In 2001 she was awarded the OBE in the Queen's Birthday Honours List

- In 2002 Arlene Philips was the Choreographer for both the Opening and Closing Ceremonies of the Commonwealth Games in Manchester
- Ariene stepped into the world of Ballroom Dancing when she became a judge on the popular TV show *Strictly Come Dancing*
- In 2008 she was the Executive Producer and Creative Director of Choreography on '*Britannia High*', a TV series made by ITV
- She later judged on other TV dance shows including: *Strictly Dance Fever*, *Dance X* and *So You Think You Can Dance*
- In 2009 she choreographed the United Kingdom's Eurovision Song Contest entry and in the same year became a Director of Sadler's Wells Theatre
- Arlene Philips is the recipient of a Carl Alan Award for Services to Dance
- Many Choreographers specialise in a particular genre of dance, but not Arlene; she choreographs across all forms of entertainment and all forms of dance, with her credits including:

2009	Director of Choreography, *Strictly Come Dancing* live tour
2008	Creative Director of Choreography, *Britannia High*, ITV TV series
2008	Choreographer, *Flashdance*, musical theatre, UK tour 2007 Choreographer, *Grease*, musical theatre
2007	Director of Choreography, *DanceX*, BBC TV dance series
2007	Choreographer/Director, *Starlight Express*, The 3rd Dimension, UK tour, musical theatre
2006	Choreographer, *The Sound of Music*, musical theatre
2006	Choreographer, *We Will Rock You*, Las Vegas/Australia, musical theatre
2005	Choreographer/Director, *Saturday Night Fever*, London and UK tours, musical theatre
2002	Choreographer, Manchester Commonwealth Games opening and closing ceremonies
1990–2006	Choreographer for numerous television commercials and music videos
1985	Choreographer, *The Meaning of Life*, director Terry Jones, starring the *Monty Python* team, film

BRENDAN COLE

Speciality: Ballroom

The Man and His Life

- Brendan grew up in Christchurch, New Zealand where he was one of three children
- His brother and his sister now both teach dance, as does Brendan – when he has the time
- He was initially a reluctant dancer, being introduced to it by his mother. However, despite his initial reluctance he soon got the bug and was competing by the age of seven years
- After leaving school at the age of 17, he became a roof layer and builder
- During a trip to Europe to compete in the World Youth Ballroom Championships he realised that if he wanted to further his career in Ballroom Dancing then he would need to move to the UK, which he did at the age of 18
- In 1996 he teamed up with the Danish Ballroom dancer Camilla Dallerup, both on and off the dance floor
- Brendan and Camilla financed their dancing dreams with day jobs, until they were eventually offered a teaching job in Hong Kong; upon acceptance of the job they both then turned professional in the 2000
- Following the move to Hong Kong, Brendan and Camilla became the New Zealand and Asian Open Champions
- They then soon also found themselves in demand as choreographers throughout the world
- Brendan has since been a professionally involved with the phenomenally international, successful Ballroom Dancing TV shows, in which he has partnered participating celebrities in the UK version, *Strictly Come Dancing*, as well as being a judge on the New Zealand version of the same show, which is called *Dancing with the Stars*
- Following his involvement with these television shows, Brendan decided to retire from competitive dancing
- His career since this move has diversified enormously with his appearance on several reality TV shows – probably as a result of his frank and straight talking nature more than his dancing ability

- In 2007 he was reunited with Camilla Dallerup for the last time when they competed in the first ever Eurovision Dance Contest
- In 2009 Brendan hosted, choreographed and performed in the UK dancing tour *Live and Unjudged*, which showcased a variety of dancing styles created by Brendan and friends
- Brendan has several strings to his bow in that, as well as being a performer, choreographer, judge and teacher of Ballroom Dancing, he is also a columnist contributing regularly to both magazines and newspapers, a TV celebrity and stage artist, having appeared in pantomime too

BRIAN FORTUNA

Speciality: Street Style Salsa

The Man and His Life

- Brian Fortuna was born in Philadelphia, USA on the 20 September 1982
- Both his parents held titles in Ballroom and Latin Dance
- From a very young age he took classes in dance at his mother's own dance school
- He was already competing in dance competitions when he was just five years old and dancing professionally at the age of 14 years
- He is a specialist in Wheelchair Ballroom and works with the US Wheelchair Dancing Association, which was founded by his mother, Sandra Fortuna. He is a graduate of the US Wheelchair Dancing Association Instructors' Programme
- Brian has appeared as a professional dancer, partnering celebrities, on both the UK *Strictly Come Dancing* show as well as the US version, *Dancing with the Stars*
- Brian has coached and choreographed the Salsa team 'Ritmo Latino'
- He has been a United States Ten Dance finalist and a United States North American Top Teacher
- Brian works as a private dance tutor at his mother's school, Universal Dance Center, in Collingswood
- In addition to his teaching and choreography, Brian has also appeared as a featured dancer in the Oscar winning film *The Aviator*, as well as in the TV series *South Beach*

- He may be a gifted dancer but Brian Fortuna's talents don't stop there for both his interests and talents are wide and diverse. He has a fascination for outer space and cosmology; he collects baseball caps and he is also a talented linguist, speaking fluent Italian as well as conversational Russian, French, Spanish and Mandarin. Many of the top dancers speak several languages – it must be all the travelling!

BRYAN WATSON AND CARMEN VINCELJ

Speciality: Latin American

BRYAN WATSON: The Man and His Life

- Bryan Watson was born in Durban, South Africa, in 1969
- He started dancing at the age of five years at the Jack Orkin School of Dance

Bryan Watson and Carmen Vincelj.
(Reproduced with kind permission of
Bryan Watson and Carmen Vincelj)

- Bryan initially studied accountancy followed by six months working in a bank, both of which he hated with a passion
- He then took an office job working for a London catering company, purely to finance the real love of his life – dancing
- His first dance partner was Claudia Leonie with whom, between the years 1988 and 1992, he won various amateur championships
- 1992 was the year in which he turned professional
- Professional successes began when in 1993 Bryan and Claudia were finalists in the British Professional Latin American Championship
- In 1994 Claudia retired and Bryan consequently took a nine month break from competitive dancing
- It was later in the same year that he then started a new partnership with Karen Hardy and together they went on to win the UK and International Professional Latin American Championships
- It wasn't until March 1999 that Bryan began his now world famous partnership with Carmen Vincelj, followed by a career that was to become a huge success
- The start of Bryan and Carmen's success began less than just one year later when they took first place honours at the British Open Championships (Blackpool) – a title they went on to win an unprecedented seven times
- They then went onto win the World Professional Latin American Champions title an amazing nine times
- In 2007 Bryan – and Carmen – decided that the time had arrived for them to retire from competitive professional dance; he then went on to travel the world both teaching and judging
- In 2008 Bryan Watson and Carmen Vincelj made a guest appearance as a professional dancers on the popular TV show, *Strictly Come Dancing*
- In 2009 he judged both the prestigious International Dance Championship (Latin) at the Royal Albert Hall and the World Professional Latin American Dancing Championship which were held that year in Blackpool
- Bryan is fluent in Afrikaan as well as in English

CARMEN VINCELJ: The Woman and Her Life

- Carmen Vincelj was born in Stuttgart, Germany on 30 August 1972 as the only child of restaurant owners Vinko and Edeltraud
- She was educated in her native Germany
- After school, Carmen studied French, English and Economics
- Unlike most professional dancers, Carmen did not start dance classes as a toddler, nor did she even start them as a young child either. In fact, Carmen Vincelj did not actually show any interest in dance at all until 1989, when she was the grand old age – in dance training terms that is – of 17 years.
- Just one short year later year and she was already competing
- In 1996 Carmen turned professional, partnering up with Allan Tornsberg
- Together, Carmen and Allan then went on to become finalists in all the major World Professional Latin American events between 1996 and 1998
- It wasn't until 1999 that the dancing partnership of Bryan Watson and Carmen Vincelj commenced and it was in that same year that, the now famous dancing partnership, became World Champions
- Success followed success and, together with her partner, Carmen was the Latin American Dance World Champion from 1999–2007
- As well as this outstanding achievement she and Bryan are also – to date – the unprecedented seven times Blackpool Champions
- Carmen retired from competitive professional dance in the year 2007 and now, as with her former professional partner, she too travels the world both teaching and judging – in the same year as her retirement, in fact, she judged the International Dance Championship (Latin) at the Royal Albert Hall
- In 2008 Carmen Vincelj and Bryan Watson made a guest appearance, as professional dancers, on the TV show *Strictly Come Dancing*
- Carmen has co-presented the German version of *Strictly Come Dancing*, which in Germany is in fact called '*Let's Dance*'

CAMILLA DALLERUP

Speciality: Latin American

CAMILLA DALLERUP: The Woman and Her Life

- Camilla was born on 6 April 1974 in Alborg, Denmark, and lived there until she was 16 years old
- She apparently learned to walk and then immediately she learned to dance, having her first dance lesson when she was only two years old, and so Camilla certainly was an early starter
- She began competing when she was six years old, but was really supposed to be eight years old to enter that particular competition!
- She was initially trained at a stage school, the Lille Nicholaisen Academy for Performance and Dance, where she was able to study all forms of dance, as well as singing, acting and modelling too, but eventually gave up the singing and acting to concentrate on Ballroom and Latin American dancing. She then cut it down ever further to concentrate primarily on the Latin American dancing
- Whilst dancing she also studied first at the Copenhagen Business School and after that she studied law and finance to become an estate agent in Denmark, which meant that she could earn money to pay for further training and the necessary costumes
- For eight years from 1996, she partnered Brendan Cole, first for four years on the amateur circuit and then for a further four years as a professional, for in the year 2000 both she and Brendan Cole turned professional
- Camilla danced on the UK TV series of *Strictly Come Dancing*, appearing in six series in total, over a period of five years, winning the title in the year 2008 with her celebrity partner, Tom Chambers
- In the same year she announced that she was leaving the show to further her career in other areas, such as TV presenting
- In 2009 she appeared on ITV's programme *I'm a Celebrity ... Get Me Out of Here!*
- She also became a fitness and health expert through the medium of dance and in 2010 appeared as *GMTV*'s Dancing Queen, where she encouraged the nation to travel the fitness route through dance exercise and diet
- She has to date made three top ten DVDs: *Magic of Dance*, *Dance off the Inches* and her latest, *Camilla's Cardiodance Workout*

DARREN BENNETT AND LILIA KOPYLOVA

Speciality: Latin American

DARREN BENNETT: The Man and His Life

- Darren is a twin and he and his brother, Dale, were born on 14 February 1977 in Deepcar, Yorkshire
- Dancing certainly runs fast and furious through this family's veins for his parents were both professional dancers and at the time of going to press own City Limits Dance Centre in Sheffield; his twin brother Dale is also a dancer
- Darren started his dance training when he was six years old and began competing at the age of seven
- After completing his education he worked as a sales manager for a shoe company as well as dancing on the amateur circuit
- Before meeting his partner Lilia, Darren danced with the same dance partner for 14 years, only splitting from her when she decided to give up dancing
- So it was that in 1997 Dale, knowing that his twin Darren was searching for a new dance partner, introduced him to Lilia Kopylova. It was an introduction that was to change Darren's life forever
- A dancing partnership between the pair was made and five months later they won the International and British Youth Championships, an indication of what was to come
- In January of 1999 the dance partnership became a life partnership when Lilia and Darren married
- In 2003 Darren and Lilia turned professional and together they became one of Britain's greatest Latin American dance pairs
- As well as competing and appearing on TV, Darren and Lilia both teach dancing

LILIA KOPYLOVA: The Woman and Her Life

- Lilia Andreievna Kopylova was born on 18 June 1978 in Moscow, Russia
- A multi-talented young lady, Lilia may specialise in Latin American dancing but is in fact an expert in many other complementary areas too, for she is trained in both Ballet and gymnastics as well as being a Moscow

figure-skating champion, winning the Moscow Championship in figure-skating when she was just six years old

- She didn't actually begin her training in Ballroom and Latin until she was nine which, compared to many world champions, is quite late in life!
- As a teenager Lilia won several titles including including USSR Ten Dance Champion, Russian National Champion and the Italian, Danish and French Open Championships
- She left Russia, first to live in Denmark where she met Dale Bennett, Darren's twin brother
- Soon after that fateful introduction Lilia Kopylova moved to the UK and as a pair Darren and Lilia won the International and British Youth Championships
- In 1999 Lilia and Darren married, thus becoming a pair both on and off the dance floor
- In the year 2003 they turned professional and in 2004 Lilia became a British Citizen
- Lilia, as well as her partner and husband Darren, has been a very successful part of the TV phenomena *Strictly Come Dancing*
- Her fitness DVD *Latinasize* became the top fitness DVD of 2006 and in 2007 she made a follow-up called *Latinatone*

DAVID SYCAMORE AND DENISE WEAVERS

Speciality: Ballroom and Latin American

DAVID SYCAMORE: The Man and His Life

- David Charles Sycamore was born in London on 1 June 1956, as the only child of Reg and Mary Sycamore
- David's father was the proprietor of a shop dealing in television and electrical goods
- He was educated at Raynes Park High School, London, where he excelled at maths and science
- David was 10 years old when he first started dancing at Wimbledon Dance Studios, and it was in 1970 that he met Denise – who was destined to become his long term partner – at a medallist competition; they were both 14 years old at the time

David Sycamore and
Denise Weavers.
(Himawari Co., Tokyo,
Japan)

- After leaving school he worked as an audio visual aids technician in a teacher training college in Wimbledon
- The pair soon became champions on the amateur circuit, winning the British National and the British Open, as well as the World Amateur Latin Championships in 1978 and 1979
- In these same two years David and Denise also won the European and World 10 Dance Championships, proving that not only did they excel at Latin American Dancing, but also at Ballroom Dancing
- It was after winning the British Open that David and Denise then decided that the time had come for them to turn professional
- To their astonishment and delight they soon found that after this decision they were immediately in demand for demonstrations not only in England but all over the world too
- David and Denise soon established themselves among the top six Professional Latin competitors and top 12 Ballroom competitors. They

won their first World and European Professional 10 Dance Championships in 1981 and went on to win these titles a further four times each before making the difficult decision to retire from the Ballroom section order to concentrate their efforts on the Latin style

- They were successful in winning the British National Professional Latin Championship on three occasions, 1983, 1984 and 1986
- 1989 saw the introduction of a new style World Championship named 'Showdance'. In Showdance competitors are permitted to choose their own music, include previously 'forbidden lifts' and generally allowed to be more individual and expressive. And so it was that in the same year David and Denise became the first ever Latin American Showdance Champions
- For an amazing 10 years David and Denise were in the top three couples worldwide in the Latin style of dance
- They were also members of the British Team at the Open British Championships on 10 different occasions, choosing the occasion of the Team Match in May 1990 to announce their retirement from competitive dance
- They did not, however, retire from the dance world per se, for they continued to travel, giving dance demonstrations and cabaret performances on an international basis for a further 11 years after their so called retirement, so passing on their knowledge and expertise to future generations
- In 1993, and in the midst of their travels, they somehow found the time, together with five other former competitive dancers, to open a dance studio in Cheam, Surrey, called 'Dance Options'. Dance Options is unique in that it is a place where current competitors on the dance circuit can take advantage of the private lessons on offer there with a variety of top class professional dancers, or merely to use the excellent facilities available to them in which to practise
- David speaks German and is studying Japanese, which is very handy when teaching in those particular countries, and is in fact the reason for his studies
- In 2009 he compered the World Latin American Championships – a skill at which he is highly adept
- He has frequently acted as Chairman of Adjudicators at such prestigious events as the World and European Professional Ballroom and Latin championships, as well as being Master of Ceremonies on various other

occasions including the World Professional Latin Championship at the
Winter Gardens, Blackpool

- As well as lecturing at Congresses for both competitive associations and
teaching organisations, David and Denise have recorded a DVD on behalf
of the IDTA, for Professionals studying for their qualifications, and on
which they demonstrate the Ballroom Technique which accompanies the
IDTA technique book

DENISE WEAVERS: The Woman and Her Life

- Denise Elaine Weavers was born on 20 November 1956 in Northampton
as the only child of Leonard and Laura Jean Weavers
- Her mother was the proprietor of a lady and baby-wear boutique; her
father was a businessman
- Denise was educated at Ecclesbourne High School in Croydon, Surrey
where she excelled in all sports, and in particular in athletics; she also
liked anything artistic, except cooking, which she disliked intensely!
- Denise was six years old when she first started dancing at Benny Tolmeyer
School, London thus, in theory, giving her a four year head start on David!
- Like her soon to be partner, she too worked her way through the IDTA
medal examinations in Ballroom and Latin dance
- During this time Denise also had a parallel dance career, when she
trained as an ice skater. However, the decision to pursue her interest in
Ballroom Dancing further was made when she found David as a dance
partner
- About six months after she and David started dancing together, and their
partnership was established, Denise gave up ice skating
- After Denise left school she became an apprentice hairdresser; she also
designed and made her own dance dresses in order that she could present
the best possible grooming
- They soon became World Amateur Champions in Latin as well as the
European and World 10 Dance Champions, proving that not only did
they excel at Latin American Dancing, but they also excelled at Ballroom
Dancing too
- When she was 22 years old, she and David turned professional, soon
becoming hugely popular on the international demonstration circuit and
extremely successful competitive dancers too

- 1989 saw Demse and David make history when they became the first ever Latin American Showdance Champions – which was a new style World Championship
- In 1990 Denise and David retired from competitive dancing, but not from their highly successful demonstration career which they continued for several more years before winding down slightly
- In 1993 there also came a new venture into Denise and David's already busy lives, with the opening of 'Dance Options' in Cheam, Surrey, a dance studio which they co-own with five other former competitive dancers and where today's current, competitive dancers can train with various professionals or where, in fact, they can simply use the first class facilities available to them

DONNIE BURNS MBE

Speciality: Latin American

DONNIE BURNS: The Man and His Life

- Donnie Burns was born in Hamilton, Scotland, to parents who were both schoolteachers
- His parents also had a dance school where he was later to start his dance training; his mother was a well-known amateur dancer
- He started dancing at the age of six years and even at that age was smitten with Latin American dance
- At the age of 10 he was already competing overseas
- On his 12th birthday he won both the Scottish Open Junior Ballroom and Latin Championships on the same day
- As well as being a talented Latin American dancer, he was academically gifted too, achieving outstanding examination results and at the age of 11 years he passed the entrance examination to Holy Cross High School
- It didn't stop there either for Donnie Burns for it seems excelled in all areas: he played football for both his primary and secondary schools; he represented his secondary school at national level in the athletic sport of high jump; he played cricket for Motherwell Cricket Club; he was editor of his school magazine and a member of the senior debating society

- After school he went on to Glasgow University to study law, but after two years ended his studies in order to concentrate on dancing
- He went on to have an extraordinarily successful competitive career. At one stage he was the World Professional Champion on 13 consecutive occasions from 1984–1996, and then again in 1998
- He is also multilingual and can converse in four languages, which has proved very useful for someone in such international demand as an expert on Latin American Dancing
- Donnie, it would seem, is loved around the world and has been invited to Japan by the Emperor; has been a guest of the President of Lithuania as well as a guest of the Dutch Royal Family; whenever he visits Russia he is accorded VIP status and in 1994 he was presented to Her Majesty Queen Elizabeth II to receive his MBE
- Since his retirement from competitive dancing, Donnie has continued travelling the world adjudicating, demonstrating and lecturing
- In 2008 Donnie Burns married dancer Heidi Groskreutz
- His home town of Hamilton in Scotland is justifiably proud of this sportsman, year after year naming him as 'Hamilton Sportsman of the Year', and in their shopping centre hangs a banner proclaiming him 'Hamilton Sporting Legend'
- At the time of going to press Donnie Burns is also Vice-President and Chairman of the Dancesport Committee of the World Dance and Dancesport Council, which is the world governing body for Professional Competitions and Championships

IAN WAITE

Speciality: Latin American

IAN WAITE: The Man and His Life

- Ian Waite was born in Reading, Berkshire, where he also grew up
- He was initially more interested in sports than in dancing and most certainly more interested in football, rugby and tennis
- It was when his father began dancing classes at the County School of Dancing in Reading every Saturday morning and took along Ian and his

younger brother that the passion began. Ian was ten years old at the time, which is a comparatively late age to start dancing

- The former Latin American Dance Champion Mary Richardson spotted that this particular 'reluctant' dancer had real talent and so took him under her wing
- At the age of 13 Ian started on the open competition circuit and soon became the European Youth Latin American Champion
- By the time he was 14 years old he had completed all his grades in both Latin American and Ballroom Dancing; furthermore he had won almost every competition for which he had been entered
- For the next ten years he partnered Melanie Walker, with whom he represented England in many European and World Championships
- It was in 1988 that Ian appeared on BBC TV's original *Come Dancing* show
- In 1997 he turned professional and moved to Holland in order to further his training. Whilst there he won the Dutch championship
- He later teamed up with the Danish dancer Camilla Dallerup
- Ian still lives in his native Berkshire and has a thriving career as a teacher, trainer and chorographer; he has also made a dance video with Angela Ripon (*Ballroom Dancing with Angela Rippon*) and a dance documentary for the BBC
- At 6'3" Ian is one of the taller professional dancers, and taking a whopping size 12 (UK) in shoes one does wonder how he never trips over his own feet, let alone his partner's!

JAMES JORDAN AND OLA JORDAN

Speciality: Latin American

JAMES JORDAN: The Man and His Life

- James Jordan was born in Gillingham, Kent on 13 April 1978
- He grew up in the Medway area of Kent with his father Alan, a site manger for a power station, his mother Sharon and his older sister, Kelly
- Before Alan and Sharon Jordan had their children they used to teach the famous Formation team at Peggy Spencer's dance school

- James didn't begin dancing until he was 10 years old, and really wasn't all that interested initially
- He began competing at the age of 14, at first only against other local dance schools, but soon further afield
- After leaving school he financed his dance training by working in the engineering industry
- At the age of 18 he started to excel in his dancing and soon found this attracted the girls, which spurred him on all the more!
- At 21 he was all set to take a break from dancing, that is until he heard that Ola Grabowska was looking for a partner. He had first seen Ola dancing when she was just 15 years old and was taken with her amazing ability even then
- So he took just a six-month break from dancing, travelling to Poland to have a try-out with Ola. Within a period of three weeks Ola had moved to the UK and they became dance partners
- Soon she was more than just his dance partner when in October 2003 James and Ola were married. It was in the same year that they also turned professional
- The Jordans then went to live in Hong Kong for four years where they taught Latin American Dancing
- Together they soon became one of the top 12 dance couples in the world, also representing England in the World Championships
- James and Ola joined the *Strictly Come Dancing* team for Series 4
- James is a sporty individual, loving most sports, including riding his own motorbike, (a sports variety of course). He even owns a speedboat and enjoys other water sports such as water siding and wakeboarding
- James and Ola's interest and involvement in the world of dance is as diverse as their talents, for they have appeared on the *Strictly Come Dancing Live Tour*, as well as performing in showcases across the UK and Europe; they have also appeared on TV shows as well as teaching on and running dance events
- James was Head Judge and Presenter on the show Dancing on Wheels, which pairs disabled and able-bodied contestants as they learn Ballroom and Latin American Dancing

OLA JORDAN: The Woman and Her Life

- Aleksandra, 'Ola', was born on 30 September 1982 in the small Polish town of Legionowo, near Warsaw, to Janina and Dariusz Grabowska
- She has one older sister, Monika, who is a pharmacist
- Like her future husband James, Ola didn't actually start dancing until the age of 10 years old
- By the age of 12 she was taking part in – small – competitions
- 1999 was an exciting year for her, when, at 17 years old, she won the Polish Championship before going to the World Championships, where she was placed in the top 12
- Shortly after the World Championships Ola split from her regular dance partner and so was in search of a new partner when she heard from James Jordan
- In March 2000 James arrived in Poland, and so successful and immediate was their partnership that she moved to England in April of the same year
- Within six months they entered their first competition and then went onto compete all over the world. They won numerous championships and became one of the top 12 dance couples in the world as well as representing England in the World Championships
- The dancing pair married in 2003
- Together with her husband James, Ola has appeared on the TV show *Strictly Come Dancing* and as a consequence of that show on the *Strictly Come Dancing Live Tour* as well
- Ola was a judge on the TV show *Dancing on Wheels*, which pairs disabled and able-bodied contestants as they learn Ballroom and Latin Dance – husband James was Head Judge on the same programme
- Ola is very keen on yoga to keep her body toned and supple
- As a contrast to yoga she also takes part in the extreme sport of wakeboarding

KAREN HARDY

Speciality: Latin American

KAREN HARDY: The Woman and Her Life

- Karen, unlike many other champion and or professionals didn't come from a dancing background, was born in Weymouth and grew up in Bournemouth
- She left school at the age of 16 to support and fund her dancing career and so went straight into a job with Barclays International in Poole
- At school Karen excelled at needlework and so at the start of her career she was able to make a lot of own dance costumes. Ironically, she was never particularly good at running in PE, yet went on to a career which involved the intense use of her legs!
- Karen started dancing at the age of five years, but unlike most little girls who at that age want to be ballerinas and so have lessons in Ballet she was

Karen Hardy.. (Reproduced with kind permission of Karen Hardy)

drawn straight into the excitement of Ballroom and Latin dance classes at a school in Boscombe. She had fallen in love, you see, with the glamour, the sequins and the dazzling costumes which is, in fact, what inspired her to dance at such a young age

- When she was 18 Karen moved to the US where she was hugely successful on the amateur circuit, becoming both East and West Coast Amateur Champion
- In 1994 she and her new dance partner, Bryan Watson, turned professional and competed together for a total of five years, during which time she was ranked as the number one female Latin American Dancer in the world
- Karen retired from competitive dance in March 1999 when, together with dance partner Bryan, she was at the height of her competitive career, being the undefeated United Kingdom, International, British National, World Masters, Open Italian, Yankie Classic, London Open and Osaka World Trophy Champion of Latin American dance, to name but a few

The Champagne Bar at the glamorous Chelsea based Karen Hardy Studios. (Reproduced with kind permission of Karen Hardy)

- Together Karen and Bryan were also awarded 'The Most Outstanding Professional Latin American Couple' by the Ballroom Dancers Federation and, for 'services to dance', the Carl Alan Award
- Karen was also awarded Crystal Palace Teacher of the Year
- In 2001 she achieved 'something' as far removed from the glamorous world of dance as is possible, completing the Inca Trail, the most famous trek in South America, which involves not only walking – a lot – but sleeping in a tent and climbing over 4,000 metres in the Andes. Those legs may not have worked for her in her PE lessons at school, but have done her proud ever since
- In 2003 Karen married Conrad Murray, with whom she has a son, Callum, who was born in 2005. Conrad himself comes from a strong dance background in New Zealand and is a champion dancer in his own right, having danced from the age of five and achieved a number of coveted Ballroom and Latin titles across all age divisions. His mother still runs a dance studio in New Zealand

Luxurious facilities at the Chelsea based Karen Hardy Studios, where International dance champions, celebrities and even complete amateurs can take advantage of both the 5* training as well as the 5* facilities on offer there. (Reproduced with kind permission of Karen Hardy)

- In 2006 Karen, together with her celebrity partner, cricketer Mark Ramprakash, won the coveted title in series four of the hit BBC TV show *Strictly Come Dancing*
- As a natural progression from competitive dancing to teaching, Karen has now taken passing on her knowledge one step further by opening her own dance studios in London with her husband Conrad. These studios are different in that they are more of a unique five star experience in dance tuition

KRISTINA RIHANOFF

Speciality: Latin American

KRISTINA RIHANOFF: The Woman and Her Life

- Kristina (Pchenitchnykh) Rihanoff was born in arctic Siberia, Russia, in 1977, where she soon became well known for her dancing skills
- Her father is a musician and so she was surrounded by music throughout her childhood
- As well as Ballroom and Latin American Dancing Kristina also studied Ballet
- Kristina entered her first dance competition when she was just seven years old
- By the time she was 16 years old she was teaching, already passing on her skills to others
- Although dancing was her passion, she did nevertheless study hard in order to obtain a Masters Degree in tourism and hospitality
- Shortly after gaining her degree, she was invited to the United States to compete professionally
- In 2001, Kristina moved to Seattle, Washington where she successfully dedicated all of her time to professional dance competitions
- She has created a series of instructional dance DVDs
- Kristina, like many performers, has an artistic flair in various arms of the arts. For example, the time of going to press, she is writing a book on stage makeup whilst at the same time taking the photographs for the book; she frequently designs her own dance costumes too
- Kristina took part in *Strictly Come Dancing* in 2008, partnering John Sargent, and in 2009 she was paired with boxer Joe Calzaghe

MARCUS AND KAREN HILTON MBE

Speciality: Ballroom, Latin American and Ten Dance

MARCUS HILTON: The Man and His Life

- Marcus Hilton was born in 1960 in Rochdale, Lancashire, as the second child and only son of Leslie and Iris Hilton
- His father was a precision engineer and his mother a secretary; he has one sister, Judith, who is seven years his senior
- His parents enjoyed dancing too and passed on their love of dance to both Marcus and Judith
- Leslie and Iris took their dance lessons, including medal examinations, at Turners Dance Centre in Rochdale, being taught by Chris and Joan Turner. They were then joined there by their son and daughter, Marcus and Judith

Marcus and Karen Hilton.
(Reproduced with kind permission of Marcus and Karen Hilton)

- Marcus was eight years old when he started dancing. Little did anyone know then what this young boy was destined to achieve
- His sister, Judith, enjoyed dancing but not with the same passion as Marcus and so eventually gave it up to follow a career in nursing
- It could so easily have turned out differently for Marcus though, and the country could well have been robbed of both a legend and a champion. For he lived at a time when many people frowned upon little boys doing, as they saw it, 'girly' things, and so as a result he was discouraged from dancing by a well meaning teacher, until his mother stepped in that is and insisted that her son be allowed to follow his dream in peace – God love mothers everywhere!
- It must be said, though, that there were teachers at the other extreme in the life of the young Marcus Hilton, for when he was at secondary school and was offered the opportunity to dance with the British Team in Dresden, his headmaster at that time was fully supportive in encouraging him to go, even though it involved taking time off school and consequently missing some important examinations. A headmaster behaving in such a way now could well be severely reprimanded
- Marcus left Balderstone Comprehensive School, where he also excelled at athletics, football and rugby, when he was 15 years old and went on to work at the Bob Dale Dance Studio in Manchester, where he stayed for 18 months, working behind the bar whilst learning all that was involved in the day to day running of a dance school
- After this he went on to sell dance shoes before working as a ceramic tile representative, whilst all the time being financially supported by his parents as he continued his dance training
- By the time he was about 12 years old he was travelling all over the country competing at national level; Karen, meanwhile, was doing exactly the same thing and so their paths frequently crossed. Little did either know at this stage that not only had they met their future dance partners, but they had also met their future partners in life too
- Until they were around 17 or 18 though, they both danced with other partners
- It was then that fate stepped in and took a hand in their future, or perhaps it was cupid? For it was at about that time that it became obvious to all concerned that Marcus's current partner was actually too small for them

to continue dancing together at a competitive level; at the same time it transpired that his teacher, Bob Dale, and his parents had always thought that Karen would, and could, be the perfect partner for Marcus – and so the match was made

- 1978 was the year in which Marcus and Karen started competing together on the amateur circuit
- In 1982 they won the World, European and British Amateur Latin American and 10 Dance Championships
- After winning the World, European and British Amateur Latin American and 10 Dance Championships for the second year running in 1983 they then turned professional, with their first major success quickly following in 1984 when they won the British Professional Rising Star Ballroom Championship
- In 1986 Marcus Hilton and Karen Johnstone married and aptly celebrated by winning the World and European Professional 10 Dance Championship in the same year
- In 1989 they won the first ever World Professional Ballroom Segue Championship (a type of show dance competition) in Germany and from then on, until their retirement from competitive dancing, they won championship after championship
- In 1995 Marcus was pronounced 'Man of the Year' in his home town of Rochdale
- In 1997 they were awarded the MBE in the Queen's Birthday Honours List for services to dance
- 1998 arrived to see them winning the World Professional Ballroom Championship for an astounding ninth time, as well as the International Ballroom Championships for the eighth time and the British Ballroom Championships for the seventh time!
- Marcus and Karen Hilton have won almost every major professional dance championship it is possible to win. They have been champions in the European, British, and V.S. Open, the U.K. Championships, as well as the World and European Professional 10 Dance Champions and have also been World Professional Ballroom Segue Champions
- After more than 20 years together on the dance floor, Marcus and Karen Hilton retired from competitive and demonstration dancing, but continued with their contribution to the world of dance through their work as International teachers, lecturers and judges

- The year of 2001 saw the birth of a tiny Hilton when their son, Henry James, arrived in the world. He soon began to show a keen interest in dance as well as sport – like father like son – only now it is unlikely that, if he wishes to take dance more seriously, he will have to endure the social opposition his father experienced all those years ago
- Since his retirement Marcus Hilton has been in demand on the International circuit as an adjudicator, teacher and lecturer and so has taken the time to learn conversational Japanese, Italian, Russian and Chinese
- In 2008 Marcus was appointed Chairman of the British Dance Festival
- At the time of going to press he, together with his wife Karen and a consortium of other Professional dancers, runs the Starlight Dance Centre in Streatham after taking over the lease from Bill and Bobbie Irvine MBE – and they say the arts world is an easy way to earn a living!

KAREN HILTON: The Woman and Her Life

- Karen (née Johnstone) was born in 1961 in Maghull, Liverpool, as the third child of James and Anastasia Johnstone
- Her father, James, was the owner of a warehouse and distribution centre in Liverpool and her mother, Anastasia, was a housewife. She has a younger sister, Cheryl, and two older brothers, Tony and Kevin
- Karen was not the only member of the Johnstone household to have a passion for dancing as her sister Cheryl also attained great success with her partner at junior level
- Karen's inspiration to dance came from such movie legends as Gene Kelly and from watching our own national treasures, such as Bill and Bobbie Irvine and Anthony and Fay Saxton
- She started Ballet classes at the age of four, continuing until she was eleven years old
- Ballroom and Latin American Dance entered Karen's world when she was just seven years old and started classes with George Coad and Pat Thompson
- She then went on to compete in Ballroom and Latin American Dance, partnering her sister Cheryl – this is and has always been an acceptable way for girls to compete in dance competitions, due to the shortage of boy dancers. They went on to win many all girl competitions all over the country

- At the age of about twelve Karen met Marcus
- Karen was an academic young lady and attended Maricourt High School in Liverpool from where she gained – in Marcus's word – 'A collection of GCSEs and A Levels'
- She was then offered a place at university studying dance, but decided to turn it down as this would have compromised her amateur status. Instead she went on to work with her father as his secretary, his cleaner and his general helper with 'everything and anything', as is usually the case when one's father is the boss

MATTHEW CUTLER

Speciality: Latin American

MATTHEW CUTLER: The Man and His Life

- Matthew David Cutler was born in Chelmsford, Essex on 30 October 1973
- When he was four years old his family moved to Southend-on-Sea, where his education began at Earl Hall Primary School followed by Cecil Jones College Secondary School
- At the age of eight he was introduced to dancing by his mother, who used to compete in Old Time Dancing, and he immediately fell in love with Latin American Dancing
- Like so many young people when they first begin dance classes, his first class was in a church hall, and not in a huge state of the art complex
- By the time Matthew reached the age of ten he was competing
- It was at this time that his training took on a more serious tone as he travelled to Birmingham for classes in Ballroom and to Hendon for classes in Latin
- As a teenager he and his partner were England's No 1 couple and were undefeated in all major competitions
- In 1996 he married Nicole Westdyk, also a champion dancer
- In 1999 he and Nicole won the World Amateur Championship and in the same year appeared in the stage show *Burn the Floor*
- Mathew and Nicole won the World Championships, the European Championships and the International Championships

Matthew and Nicole Cutler.
(Reproduced with kind permission
of Matthew and Nicole Cutler)

- In 2003 Matthew and Nicole divorced, later reuniting as non-competitive dance partners in 2006
- In 2007 Matthew partnered Alesha Dixon when she won the TV show/ competition *Strictly Come Dancing*
- Matthew has twice received the Carl Alan Award for outstanding contribution to dance

VINCENT SIMONE AND FLAVIA CACACE

Speciality: Latin American, Ballroom and Argentine Tango

VINCENT SIMONE: The Man and His Life

- Vincent was born in Foggia, Southern Italy, on 15 March 1979, into a 'dancing family'

Vincent Simone and Flavia Cacace.
(Credit vincentandflavia.com)

- His mother Anna and father Gaspare Simone are themselves professional Ballroom and Latin dancers, as well as teachers of dance; his sister, Alessandra, also teaches dance – Street Dance and Hip Hop
- He was born to be natural show-off, taking any opportunity to perform from the outset
- Vincent is just six inches short of being six foot tall
- He was only 12 years old when he started teaching dance in Italy and he has continued to enjoy teaching ever since
- By the time he was 16 years old he was the Italian Youth Champion
- He moved to England at the age of 17, basing himself in Guildford, Surrey. It was here that he met his partner, Flavia, who by strange coincidence is also Italian. The two Italian dancers then became an Italian dancing pair
- Vincent is a world expert in the Argentine Tango

- In 2009 Vincent Simone became a father when his son, Luca, was born
- He has another two passions in his life, in addition to dance: *fast* cars and computers

FLAVIA CACACE: The Woman and Her Life

- Flavia was born in Naples, Italy on 13 March 1980 as the youngest child in a family of six
- Her father, Roberto, who was at the time a chef, together with his wife Rosaria moved the family to Surrey when Flavia was just four years old
- In England she was educated at four Guildford schools: Sandfields, St Thomas's Primary Catholic School, St Peter's Comprehensive, finally completing her education in 1995 at Guildford College
- She met her Italian dance partner, Vincent Simone, at a dance school in Surrey when she was 16 years old and, at the suggestion of their dance teacher, the two paired up
- At a tiny 5'2" Flavia was the perfect height for her Vincent
- In 2001 Flavia Cacace and Vincent Simone turned professional
- Most professional dancers excel in one field or the other, either Latin or Ballroom, but not Flavia and Vincent for they were the UK 10 Dance Professional Champions for four consecutive years and are exceptional in both fields
- Flavia and Vincent's, greatest love is the Argentine Tango and in 2005 they won the World Championships. Since then they have developed spectacular show dances which they have performed both on TV and at events all over the UK
- Both have reached the finals of the TV show *Strictly Come Dancing*
- Flavia is an animal lover and says that if she wasn't dancing then she would probably enjoy working with animals

Chapter 5

THE MORE POPULAR DANCES

I thought this section would be straightforward when I set about writing it. What could be simpler than a brief description of the most popular dances? Well I tell you what could be simpler – most things on the planet, it would seem! I like black and white, a beginning with an end, a question with an answer. Not much to ask, is it? Well, in the world of Ballroom Dancing, it would seem that it is far too much to ask! This is a subject with more twists and turns than a Viennese Waltz, and furthermore this is an end with no beginning. Like anything 'arty', dance is open to interpretation and is subjective in the extreme – which, of course, only serves to make it all the more fascinating, and of course frustrating too, at times even confusing. As far as the background to each dance is concerned then the theories tend to differ wildly in some cases, and so I have had to tread a somewhat middle ground. I do hope though that you will find this section as interesting to read as I have found it fascinating to research and write.

So, in no particular order as the saying goes, except but alphabetical of course, I will start with the romantic American Smooth.

AMERICAN SMOOTH

A Ballroom Dance which breaks the rules of close contact

THE BACKGROUND TO THE AMERICAN SMOOTH

- The American Smooth is a form of Ballroom Dancing which complies with all the basic principles and techniques of Ballroom Dancing with which we are familiar, except in the fact that in this dance continuous body contact is not required, as it is in all the other Ballroom Dances – so I suppose, in fact, that this is the dance which *doesn't* comply at all with the basic principles and techniques! And so we start as we mean go on, in a confusing and contradictory manner

- The American Smooth takes steps from standard Ballroom Dances, with the exception of the Quickstep, to create a new and exciting interpretation
- This is a dance which goes back to the wonderful Hollywood musicals featuring Fred Astaire and Ginger Rogers and is more elaborate than the more traditional of Ballroom Dances

CHARACTERISTICS OF THE AMERICAN SMOOTH

- The American Smooth has a larger repertoire of dance steps than the standard Ballroom Dances
- Generally this dance incorporates steps from the three Ballroom disciplines of the Waltz, the Viennese Waltz and the Foxtrot
- In the American Smooth dancers can perform steps such as underarm turns, dips and drops, side by side positions, parallel turns and other such steps not normally permitted in Ballroom Dancing
- Lifts are also allowed in the American Smooth, but with a maximum of only two; shuffles are also often included
- Posture should be erect and elegant, both in and out of hold
- Dance partners must be in hold for only 40 per cent of the dance, with the added bonus that it actually doesn't matter at what stage, and neither does it have to be continuous
- There should be a seamless transition from hold to release and back again with all movements having a feeling of fluidity

ARGENTINE TANGO

A story telling dance of raunchy passion

BACKGROUND TO THE ARGENTINE TANGO

- This is apparently the story of a gaucho (a South American cowboy) who, after riding his horse across the pampas, strides into town. In the local bar he meets up with a local woman of dubious reputation
- The Argentine Tango spread to Europe in the early 20th century and by 1913 had become a worldwide phenomenon
- Considered to be a very raunchy dance, a 'cleaner' version was created, which became known as the Ballroom Tango

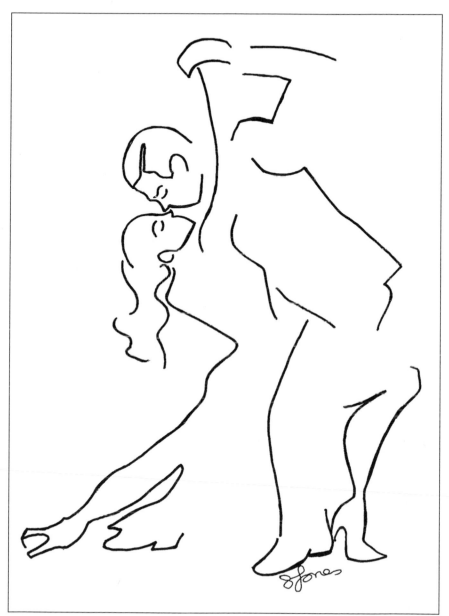

ARGENTINE TANGO – an exhilarating dance with dramatic lifts and drops which at one time was banned but is now increasingly popular. (Reproduced with kind permission of the artist Stephanie Jones)

CHARACTERISTICS OF THE ARGENTINE TANGO

- This very raunchy dance is the story of a relationship between a man and a woman and it is essential in the Argentine Tango that the dancers tell a story through their dancing
- In keeping with the style and suggestive nature of the dance, the hold is much tighter and closer than is usual
- It is more sensual and more intimate than the Ballroom Tango with the couple's upper bodies close together throughout the dance, whilst their lower bodies are apart. In the lower body the dance moves are frenetic, whilst the upper body remains calm and static
- Intricate foot and leg work is required as a part of this dance
- Kicks and flicks are a huge part of the character of the Argentine Tango and, as a part of the raunchy feel, should be executed between each partner's legs, with added dragging and jumping moves; strong leg lines are essential
- In this dance the woman's left hand is placed lower than usual, the reason for this being that she is supposedly checking for a wallet in his pocket!
- The woman also sometimes runs the toe of her foot up her partner's leg and to his pocket, again supposedly to check for the feel of coins in his pocket
- An interesting note here is that there are two forms of Argentine Tango. There is the *Social* Argentine Tango, in which there are no lifts and drops, and then there is the *Exhibition* Argentine Tango, which includes all the complicated stuff!

BALLROOM TANGO

An aggressive Ballroom Dance of control and power, rather than a dance of elegance

BACKGROUND TO THE BALLROOM TANGO

- The Ballroom Tango is said to have had its birth in the late 19th century ghettos of Argentina
- An interesting point to note here is that the Tango used to be a Latin American Dance and the Jive used to be a Ballroom Dance, but, as with

BALLROOM TANGO – Here we have a move called a contra check for the aggressive Ballroom Tango. (Reproduced with kind permission of the artist Stephanie Jones)

everything else, things change with the passing of time. The reason for the change in the case of these two dances was because the Tango was the only one of the Latin Dances that wasn't free whilst the Jive was the only Ballroom Dance that was taken out of hold – and so it was that the dances were, quite rightly, swapped over and the Tango became a member of the Ballroom family with the Jive being adopted into the Latin family

- It was in the second decade of the 20th century that the Ballroom Tango was introduced to British dancers

CHARACTERISTICS OF THE BALLROOM TANGO

- You could be forgiven for thinking that the Argentine Tango and the Ballroom Tango are similar, but to be honest if they are danced correctly then this shouldn't be the case, for there are very distinct differences
- Unlike the Argentine Tango the general hold in the Ballroom Tango is compact and the couple dance tightly together in a fixed, almost regimental style
- During this dance the woman holds her head back and prominently to the left, away from the man
- There is very little elegance in this dance, and certainly none of the elegance of the rise and fall, for it is a very flat dance as well as being a dance of aggression
- It is also a dance of dramatic positions, where all the movements should be sharp and staccato with rigid and severe lines
- During the promenade position in the Ballroom Tango, the woman's head must move very sharply from left to right
- The man's knees should be fixed in a stalking movement with sharp and jabbing feet; slow and deliberate walks should be executed in the style of someone stalking their prey and should be alternated with sudden, fast actions
- The Ballroom Tango is the epitome of drama and aggression

CHA CHA

A Latin American fast, fun, flirty and a cheeky dance

BACKGROUND TO THE CHA CHA

- This is the 'baby' of the Latin Dances in that it is a relative newcomer, having evolved in Cuba in the 1940s, not making its debut onto the dance floors of America until the 1950s
- For the Cha Cha (or Cha Cha Cha as it was originally known), as with most dances in both the Ballroom section and the Latin American section, there are many stories surrounding the birth of the dance, but most would agree that the name actually comes from the sound of the rhythm made by the dancer's feet on the floor and that it evolved from the Mambo, it actually being a triple Mambo
- The name Cha Cha is onomatopoeic meaning that it echoes the sound of the dancer's feet on the floor
- We cannot say that there are actually variations of this dance, more relations. As an example it is very close in style to both the Rumba and the Samba

CHARACTERISTICS OF THE CHA CHA

- This is a cheeky dance and should be full of fun with lots of booty and leg action and a general feel of 'Catch me if you can!' about it
- It is a dance all about sensual rhythms with small steps and lots of hip action, with a fun and flirty feel
- It is slower in rhythm than the Mambo and less complicated too
- When dancing the Cha Cha think: 'left, right, cha cha cha; right, left, cha cha cha', which creates the distinctive syncopation of the dance, where five steps are danced to four beats
- The movements should be smooth and not jerky, as often happens with beginners
- Lines should be long, strong and dynamic and toes turned out; there should be lots of changes of shape too
- Partners dance opposite each other rather than in a clasped hold, dancing generally with just the hands touching

A basic step of both the Rumba and the Cha Cha. (Reproduced with kind permission of the artist Stephanie Jones)

- This is a dance that can move forward without even a step being taken, with the characteristic movements often being in the hips or shoulders
- The timing for this dance starts on the second beat of the bar
- The New Yorker is a step frequently used in the Cha Cha
- The music for the Cha Cha is fun music with a distinct Latin feel and is generally in 4/4 time, although sometimes it is in 2/4 time with, ideally, a tempo of 32 bars per minute; however, it is often played more quickly than this
- The melodic notes for this dance are generally played staccato

FOXTROT

The dance loved by the experts and feared by everyone else

BACKGROUND TO THE FOXTROT

- One story, telling of the origin of the Foxtrot is – to me – one of the most interesting and goes like this: American Vaudeville star, Harry Fox, was dancing on the roof of New York's converted theatre, Jardin de Danse, where he was unable to find female dancers who could do the difficult Two Step. So, to solve the problem, he introduced two 'trots', and so his dance became known as Fox's Trot
- At that point in time the dance was faster and closer in tempo to the Quickstep than it is today
- They say that this is *the* dance for *real* dancers, probably because it is open to so many interpretations for what is essentially such a simple dance; whatever the reason, it is certainly the favourite of many amateur and professional dancers

CHARACTERISTICS OF THE FOXTROT

- For the Foxtrot the dancers must be very relaxed, whilst remaining in perfect control as they smoothly flow around the floor, with all of the movements blending into one continuous glide
- The appearance given should be of gliding across the floor with a smooth rise and fall. So, when it is your chance to show what you can do with the Foxtrot, then just imagine that you are Fred and Ginger floating off into the sunset, and all will be well with the dance!

FOXTROT – The dance for dancers; everyone wants to learn the Foxtrot, but few succeed! (Reproduced with kind permission of the artist Stephanie Jones)

- Steps taken forwards or sideways are usually taken on the ball of the foot
- Good posture is essential in this seemingly easy but very difficult dance and a tendency to lift the shoulders to achieve this must be avoided. A strong frame throughout is essential, making sure that there is a nice swing and sway with the body
- The woman's body should lean slightly backwards from the waist up, in a very relaxed manner
- The Foxtrot requires the dancers to shift constantly from the ball to the heel of the foot – turning on the balls and pivoting on the heels
- During this dance the dancers should make good use of the floor and cover it well, as they work in zigzags
- The music for the Foxtrot is in 4/4 time, that is four even beats per bar of music, with the tempo varying between slow and fast

JIVE

The dance of youth, it is fun, free, wild and energetically extreme

BACKGROUND TO THE JIVE

- Often perceived incorrectly as a new dance the truth is that the origin and actual birth is, quite frankly, unknown, but it was certainly around in the 19th century
- The Jitterbug, Rock 'n' Roll and the Jive are all an incestuous and confusing part of the same family and Rock 'n' Roll grew out of the rhythm and blues music played by the black musicians of the 1920s in the US, quickly becoming the dance of the young, with the older generation disapprovingly trying to ban it from the dance halls. Just as the earlier versions of the Waltz, the Jive outraged common decency!
- The Jive was brought to the UK by the GIs in the Second World War, and wherever they were stationed they taught the dance to the locals. As well as the Ballrooms and dance halls the local village halls would hold regular Saturday night 'bops' where the young would gather together and dance away the fear of the war, with all the abandon that this seemingly wild dance required

CHARACTERISTICS OF THE JIVE

- This is a fun dance and so smiling is an essential ingredient; if the dancers don't look as though they are having the time of their lives, then the dance just won't work – it's as simple as that! And let's face it, everyone can smile, even if not dance to a great standard!
- Body positioning is essential and the dancers should reach forward energetically, with knees up high to the rib cage
- The feel of this dance should be one of freedom with fancy footwork and boundless energy
- Everything about this dance should give a feel of relaxation; the hold is similar to that of the Samba, though the arms are held a little lower – just above the waist and with bent elbows – with the man holding the lady's left hand in his right hand
- The Jive should be a fast and energetic dance, with fast kicks and flicks
- Remember that kicks come from the hip and flicks come from the knee
- Leg positions are often symmetrical; arms are loose and expressive, though not with the total freedom to fling about just anywhere and in any manner as can sometimes happen!
- There is no body contact in this dance and so the guide from the man comes through his hands. It is also acceptable for the man to indicate moves to his partner via a mixture of visual and verbal signals
- This is a non-progressive dance, being danced in its 'home' space
- Fancy footwork can include the feet turning outwards in the chicken walk and flicking from the ankle
- The Jive is more dependent upon the accents in the music, particularly the second and fourth beat in the bar, than its sedate Ballroom relatives
- There is usually a prominent beat, that runs through the very heart of the music used for this dance, and one that never lets up too

THE JIVE is a fast and flashy dance which was brought to the UK by the GIs during the Second World War. (Reproduced with kind permission of the artist Stephanie Jones)

LINDY HOP

The dance that broke through the race barriers of the 1920s and 1930s

BACKGROUND TO THE LINDY HOP

- The Lindy Hop is generally considered to be the father of all Swing dances and evolved in the 1920s and 1930s of Harlem, New York, together with the jazz music of that era
- It is said that this dance was named after Charles Lindbergh's flight to Paris in 1927, when the newspaper headline read LINDY HOPS THE ATLANTIC
- The Lindy Hop could be called a social dance in more ways than one, for it broke through the race barriers which still existed at the time of its evolvement, when segregation was still considered acceptable, normal even
- It is a blend of the African rhythms and movements together with the European approach to structured dance form

CHARACTERISTICS OF THE LINDY HOP

- Despite the name of this dance, there is no actual 'hop' in it and so, defying its name, it is a smooth, flowing dance in style
- It is also known as the Jitterbug or the Lindy
- The Lindy Hop often includes aerial jumps and so can be described as an athletic style of dance and is certainly not for the feint hearted, or couch potato for that matter, for it can be wild with frenetic twists, flips, kicks and body movements. On the other hand, however, it can be slow and sophisticated and on those occasions is often described as a gentle dance, smooth and flowing in style. Whichever, it is always precise and at one with the music
- The Lindy Hop, which is based on earlier dances such as the Charleston and the Black Bottom and on Tap Dancing, is generally danced to jazz music from the late 1920s to the 1940s and to the big band music popular at that time
- For the basic step of the swingout one needs to remember that in the open position the partners are connected hand-to-hand whereas in the closed position the partners are connected as though embracing
- This is a dance in which the dancers can actually improvise

MAMBO

Generally considered the mother of the other Latin Dances

BACKGROUND TO THE MAMBO

- As with the history behind all dances – and it would seem in particular with the Latin dances – there is great variation on the many theories and stories told as to the origin of the Mambo
- One theory is that it evolved from the rhythms of the dances performed by the Cuban sugar cane cutters out in the fields
- In the mid-1950s the Mambo was a huge dance craze in the Havana clubs of that period
- It has enjoyed a revival in popularity in recent years thanks to singers such as Ricky Martin

CHARACTERISTICS OF THE MAMBO

- The feeling for the Mambo is not in the hips, as one would expect of a Latin Dance, but in the knees and the feet
- It is, as with most Latin Dances, a very sensual dance and it is said that the term 'shake it' was first coined as a result of the hip movements in the dance
- One interesting feature of the Mambo is that there is one step in every bar where the dancer actually takes no step at all, but instead rests
- When moving forwards and backwards the dancers must sway their hips
- The steps for the Mambo are very small and rhythmic and are worked flat on the balls of the feet
- Music for the Mambo is a combination of Latin and jazz rhythms and this rhythm is set by the use of percussive instruments, including maracas and cowbells
- The tempo for this dance is very fast, which makes it one of the more difficult of the Latin Dances

PASO DOBLE

A dance of sheer elegance, displaying Flamenco moves

BACKGROUND TO THE PASO DOBLE

- The Paso Doble is different to the other dances in the Latin family in that it does not have its roots in Africa but actually comes from Spain with the name meaning 'two step'
- This is a dance with a purpose in that it tells the story of a bullfight, in which the man generally represents the matador and the woman the cape. Some interpretations of the Paso Doble, however, depict the woman as the bull, and in other interpretations even as the matador or a as dancer
- The difference between the two main interpretations is that in the first, where the woman portrays the cape, she is often required to flow elegantly and fluidly across the dance floor, whereas in the second interpretation, where she portrays the bull, she is required to adopt a more aggressive and dramatic approach to the dance
- Whatever the interpretation though, this is a dance of pure story-telling

CHARACTERISTICS OF THE PASO DOBLE

- Strong, powerful and dominant Flamenco movements are required for the Paso Doble
- Posture is more important in this dance than in any of the other Latin Dances, with the man tall and proud, his chest out and his bum tucked under
- The Paso Doble does not stay 'home', but travels around the dance floor
- There should be lots of drama, passion and even aggression in this dance
- When the interpretation dictates that the woman plays the part of the bull then aggression and dramatic poses should come into play
- The feet in this dance are used to attract the attention of the bull and the walks should have strong heel leads
- The feel of the Flamenco, with the simulated use of castanets, drives through and influences the style of this dance
- It is danced to the march music used for processions at the beginning of a corrida

PASO DOBLE – A bullfight on the dance floor! (Reproduced with kind permission of the artist Stephanie Jones)

QUICKSTEP

A sweeping, flamboyant and exhilarating dance littered with hops, tricks and quick, fun steps

BACKGROUND TO THE QUICKSTEP

- The mother and father of the Quickstep was in fact the Foxtrot, with the Quickstep evolving in the jazz era of the 1920s at a time when many bands actually played the slow Foxtrot too fast, the result of this being that there were then two basic forms to the Foxtrot – the *Quick* and *Slow* Foxtrots
- And so it was that the fast Foxtrot was known in Britain as the Quick-Time Foxtrot, which soon became known by the shorter name of the Quickstep
- The Foxtrot then had developed into two completely different dances, ie the Foxtrot and the Quickstep
- The Quickstep was greatly influenced by the Charleston and good, experienced Ballroom Dancers still incorporate some Charleston figures into their dances

CHARACTERISTICS OF THE QUICKSTEP

- There are two basic movements in this dance, the walk and the chassé, with all the basic figures built upon these two movements
- The chassé steps are, in fact, synonymous with the name Quickstep and, although they can be danced in different ways, they are always made up of three steps and counted as 'quick, quick, slow'. Taking four beats of the music the feet are always closed on the second of the three steps
- We must be aware that the Quickstep is in fact all about the tricky, fancy, fast moving footwork
- Despite the speed of this dance there should be an overall feeling of elegance and the dancers should be light on their feet as they skip, trip and almost run across the floor, giving the impression that they are flying across the dance floor with their feet looking as though they barely touch the floor itself
- The upper body must appear calm and serene, whilst the feet must point on all kicks
- Because the music is up-tempo, it is essential that the steps are kept small in order to keep time
- The music should be light hearted, fun and quick

QUICKSTEP – A Dance based on the Charleston incorporating lots of flicks and hops.
(Reproduced with kind permission of the artist Stephanie Jones)

RUMBA

A dance of romance, sexual passion and rhythm

BACKGROUND TO THE RUMBA

- Like many dances, there are many stories surrounding its birth, but most would seem to agree that the Rumba dates back to African ritual dances transported to the New World by the slave trade
- It would appear that, along with the Cha Cha, the Rumba was born in Cuba, where it surfaced in its modern form in the late 19th century
- The Rumba, like many Latin Dances and indeed even like some Modern Ballroom Dances, was initially condemned for its sexual nature
- A less sexual version became more accepted, however, in the 1930s and from there its popularity grew, although to this day it remains a dance of female domination and seduction, which in essence makes it a difficult dance for the more inhibited of female dancers
- The slower tempo of the Spanish Bolero was a great influence in the development of the Rumba

CHARACTERISTICS OF THE RUMBA

- In this dance the woman is attempting to dominate the man with her feminine charms
- As with all Latin Dances it is necessary to concentrate on the upper and lower body as though they are two different components – the upper body delivers the musicality of the dance whilst the lower body delivers the rhythm and feel of the piece
- The dancers must go from ball flat into the ball of the foot and with no walking on the heels
- A sexy hip action is an essential element in this dance, and remember that the hip movement must come from the leg, with the straightening of the legs making the hips work
- This is a passionate and romantic dance and so a romantic connection and interplay between the couple must be evident during the execution of the Rumba
- This is a non-progressive dance, meaning that it is danced on the 'home space'

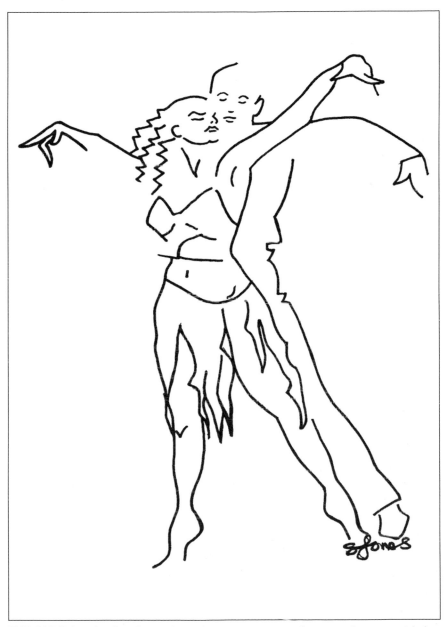

THE RUMBA – In this dance the woman attempts to dominate the man with her feminine charms. (Reproduced with kind permission of the artist Stephanie Jones)

- Shifting the weight from one leg to another thrusts the hips from side to side; the resting leg then extends to accentuate the lines
- Because this dance starts on the second beat of the bar, beginners find it extremely difficult, and so for this reason teachers frequently put in an extra side step to start on the first beat
- This is the only slow dance within the Latin American family of dances

SALSA

A hot, spicy and saucy dance

BACKGROUND TO THE SALSA

- It's not easy to place geographically, or indeed attribute, this dance to anywhere or anyone specific, for it appears to be an amalgamation of various dance styles of various origins. It is almost a distillation of many Latin and Afro-Caribbean dances, each playing its own part in the birth of the Salsa, and so in the Salsa can be found elements of the Samba, Mambo and Cha–Cha
- It is not a dance usually performed at competitions and so even professional dancers can sometimes struggle with the complexities of style

CHARACTERISTICS OF THE SALSA

- The Salsa is a dance of courtship
- With salsa, meaning sauce, it goes to follow then that the Salsa dance should be a hot and spicy dance
- This is a dance where both partners should shine in equal measure, though the man must lead and the lady follow in traditional Ballroom style
- The hold for the Salsa should be close with the man's left hand and the woman's right hand held at eye level; the man's right hand should be around the waist of the woman and the woman's left hand around the man's neck or, alternatively, around his back
- Dancers need rhythmically smooth hips for this dance. There's lots of hip action, yes, but it must be smooth and sensual hip action

THE SALSA – as saucy as its name, this dance has its roots in the clubs of Cuba. (Reproduced with kind permission of the artist Stephanie Jones)

- The Cuban Salsa is the most original form of Salsa and was created by the Cuban immigrants in New York, who mixed Salsa with elements of Rock 'n' Roll
- The Salsa should sizzle with accentuated body movement and rolls, with the legs moving at speed with a loose flexibility, whilst the hand and arm movements have a stylised feel to them
- The Salsa lends itself to improvisation, which makes for even more excitement; but for some, however, this makes it even more difficult to master and perform
- It is a dance of seduction and for that very reason direct eye contact is essential, along with the close hold
- Generally speaking, Salsa music will interestingly include some African rhythms
- When dancing this dance in the Salsa clubs that have recently sprung up worldwide, changing partners is the norm making this social dance *very* sociable

SAMBA

*An explosive, lively, flirtatious and exciting dance with a party –
Mardi Gras – feel*

BACKGROUND TO THE SAMBA

- This is the national dance of Brazil, of which many versions are danced at the Carnival in Rio
- In fact the Samba is now the hub of the Rio Carnival, which is held each year to mark the beginning of Lent, and in which the Samba schools flamboyantly parade the streets
- The Samba comes from a melting pot of three different cultures: African rhythms, Portuguese songs and Indian rituals
- In 1939 the Samba was introduced into the US by Carmen Miranda
- In the same year it was performed at the World Exhibition, New York, heralding its popularisation in films such as *That Night in Rio* and *Flying Down to Rio*

CHARACTERISTICS OF THE SAMBA

- The Samba is a flirtatious party dance with a lot of bounce and wiggle and so good hip action is an essential ingredient to its success
- Generally, Latin Dances are clipped in style, but not so the Samba, which involves the couple dancing in unison
- The accent in this dance is on the straight and extended legs and arms
- It is generally considered to be the most difficult of the Latin Dances because usually in the Latin family the dances have the same rhythm throughout, whereas in the Samba there are different rhythms, giving it that great, exciting and unique flavour
- The hold for this dance varies to that in standard Ballroom Dances in that the man's left arm is held a little higher and his left hand is on about a level with the top of his left ear. The lady's left hand should be placed on the man's right shoulder
- For most of this dance, the couples dance slightly apart
- The feet are used as brakes in the fast turns
- A slight downward bouncing or dropping action, achieved through flexing and straightening of the knees, is characteristic of the Samba
- The man takes the lead by using both of his arms
- It is the hip rotation that moves the dancer from foot to foot and in turn creates the carnival feel to the dance
- Generally this dance is executed on the ball of the foot with everything soft and cushioned to create the lovely flowing movement of the dance; the heel must not hit the ground hard, but slowly in a cushioned landing
- Ballroom Dances generally travel around the floor, whereas the Latin Dances stay 'home', with the exception of the Paso Doble and the Samba, which do travel around the dance floor
- This is a carnival/party dance with a taste of the Mardi Gras which should be evident in the general feel of the dance
- The Samba ends dramatically with the throwing back of the heads and arms splayed out to the side

THE SAMBA – A Latin dance which travels around the room. (Reproduced with kind permission of the artist Stephanie Jones)

VIENNESE WALTZ

A dance of fast and excessive whirls and twirls

BACKGROUND TO THE VIENNESE WALTZ

- The Viennese Waltz can be traced back to the 12th century, where it can be found in a dance called the Nachtanz
- This is one of the most difficult dances to conquer, quite simply because of the speed required
- When one thinks of and visualises the Viennese Waltz, what generally springs to mind is glorious and romantic images of the aristocracy in Vienna dancing to the music of Strauss

CHARACTERISTICS OF THE VIENNESE WALTZ

- A graceful dance of turns, and not just one or two either, but turn after turn after turn with not a single straight line to be danced
- This is a surprisingly fast dance – even faster than the Quickstep – and with the constant turns can make the dancers feel quite dizzy
- The Viennese dance is one in which the hold should never change – to be honest, I don't think most dancers would dare let go for a second anyway for fear of falling!
- Because of the speed of the dance there is little room for error and the legs in particular have to be in the right place at the right time, with each partner's knees slightly to the right of the other partner's, to avoid any painful knocking!
- Unlike the majority of Ballroom Dances, which have numerous steps to learn, the Viennese Waltz has by comparison very few steps/moves to learn, there being just three in fact: there is the natural turn, which is a turn to the right, a reverse turn, which is a turn to the left and in between the two there is a change step
- The rise and fall of the standard Waltz is still necessary but, because of the speed of this dance, not quite so many
- Footwork must be precise with swing and sway as a part of the posture and hold

- The music for the Viennese Waltz is like the English Waltz and as in ¾ time, only this time it is at double the speed and played at about 60 bars a minute
- One interesting fact is that although the music is in 3/4 time, the second beat is more hurried, thus giving the dance its Viennese, romantic lilt in the movement

WALTZ

Elegant and graceful, this is a dance which epitomizes romance and exudes grace

BACKGROUND TO THE WALTZ

- Although difficult to pinpoint with definitive accuracy, it is generally considered that the Waltz is a dance with an international ancestry, possibly having evolved from 18th century European folk dances and is one of the oldest of the Ballroom Dances
- In the 18th century it grew and spread across Europe and by the mid-19th century had arrived in America
- It was at the beginning of the 19th century that the Waltz, with its modern hold, finally took root in England. It was not, however, welcomed and hailed as a great success but more as a dance of profanity, for it was considered an outrageous affront to common decency for a man and a woman to dance so closely together and so as a consequence it was generally known as the 'forbidden dance'. Louis XIII of France (1601–1643) had previously banned it from his court for this very reason
- The Waltz continued to be given the cold shoulder until, it is said, the Emperor Alexander of Russia was seen waltzing around the room. Later Queen Victoria helped push forward the social acceptability of the Waltz, for she was herself an excellent Ballroom Dancer and felt a great affinity with this particular dance; as a result of its Royal connections it gained the respectability it had hitherto been denied
- The Waltz may have been around for a long time but the English Waltz as we know it today didn't actually start until around the 1920s, when the Imperial Society of Teachers of Dancing standardised the moves

CHARACTERISTICS OF THE WALTZ

- The Waltz is a graceful and smooth dance with a lot of rotation, and a dance in which the hold should never change. A dance of turns may look graceful whilst spinning around the room, but trying to keep one's balance is an art all in itself! It is not an easy for anyone, especially the beginner
- The Waltz requires the classic Ballroom hold, which is: the woman must be placed slightly to the man's right, with her left hand on his upper arm and his right hand on her shoulder blade
- For this dance the most important rule is simple for when executing the steps, the dancer must never use the same foot twice in a row
- The basic rule observed then, the major characteristic can come into play, and that is the rise and fall. The rise and fall in the Waltz gives it all the elegance one expects from this dance. It is a technique used in other dances, of course, but in the Waltz it is far more pronounced and therefore obvious as the dancers rise onto their toes at the end of each bar of music and then smoothly lower their heels to start the next bar. Remember too, that the heel must lead on the first beat of the music
- Symmetry is important in the Waltz and so for this reason the position of the partners' legs frequently mirror each other
- Elbows should be high and in line with the shoulders all the way through the dance
- In comparison to other Ballroom Dances, the Waltz has very few steps – in fact it has only three! Simplicity doesn't, however, translate into easy, for in fact when one thinks sensibly about it, the fewer steps on display must surely then make it easier to spot the mistakes!
- The Waltz uses a change step to help the dancers move from one foot to the other in between the natural and reverse steps
- Close body contact is maintained throughout the execution of the Waltz – which is, of course, why it was initially thought to be an immoral dance.
- There should be a sway of the body to the side and the shoulders should swing into turns during the Waltz
- Originally the music for the Waltz was quite fast, but it is now slow, melancholic and romantic in a gentle and easily recognised time signature of ¾ time
- To achieve the maximum and romantic effect, music with a strong melody should be used for the Waltz

THE WALTZ – The easiest and oldest of all the Ballroom Dances, this is the only dance in ¾ time. (Reproduced with kind permission of the artist Stephanie Jones)

VARIATIONS OF THE WALTZ

Interestingly, and just to complicate matters, there are several variations of the Waltz:

- **The Viennese Waltz,** which is danced to music at a tempo of just under 60 bars a minute, is more simple in its execution than the English Waltz, but is quite beautiful to watch, especially when the dance floor is full of twirling dancers
- **The Old Time Waltz** is a dance which is based on the five positions of the foot in Ballet and is now popular in the Old Time Dance Clubs and as a part of many Sequence Dances
- **The Boston Waltz** was an American version of the Waltz and was popular at the end of the 19th and beginning of the 20th century

Chapter 6

LOOKING FOR INFORMATION?

allroom Dancing is no different to any other dance form, or any other subject for that matter, in that it is a treasure trove of fascinating information and facts for those who are interested and, as you are reading this book, then I assume it is fair to say that you must be interested in Ballroom Dancing to a lesser or greater degree and so this section is, therefore, for you. Browse it, dip in and out, or settle down for a straight-through read; whatever approach you decide to take, then I hope that here you will find the answers to your questions, and even the answers to questions you had never even thought about until you saw the answers! But more than that – I hope that this section will stimulate your interest in Ballroom Dancing for you to take it on to the next level.

AN OVERVIEW OF BALLROOM DANCES

Ballroom Dancing is social dancing. The word 'ball' is from the Latin word ballare, which means 'to dance'

There is more to Ballroom Dancing than just the popular and well-know competitive dances, such as the Waltz and the Quickstep. For Ballroom Dancing, in all its glory, is actually a treasure trove of dances from the popular to the specialist, the quaint to the outrageous, and from the new to the old, the sophisticated to the free; it's all there for the taking, as they say. But over a period of time the outsider has come to believe that it consists of just these few well known dances that the media feed to us when they are reporting on competitions or broadcasting for the masses. Social dancing is, though, as international and diverse as humanity itself.

Why then, do we seem to think of it as just a collection of a few popular dances? Well, to understand how this has come about one has to remember that Ballroom Dancing is a competitive sport and so, of course, is governed by rules and regulations, one of those being that only certain dances qualify to be admitted into the 'Ballroom Club', and then added to that, those restrictions, rules and regulations also differ from country to country, thus making it a minefield for the inexperienced. *The Pocket Guide to Ballroom Dancing*, however, is not a competitive book and so I have chosen throughout to select other well known dances rather than the qualifying dances specific to any competition rules in any country. Taking the words 'Ballroom Dance' as an umbrella term rather than a specific term, as in 'Dancesport', and remembering that any social dance can be called a Ballroom Dance, then below you will find an additional selection of dances for you just to browse and enjoy, with a very brief description of each.

Allemande
A courtly, baroque-style processional dance which was fashionable in the 16th century and in which the dancers form a line of couples, extend their paired hands forward and then proceed to 'walk' up and down the Ballroom.

Bailatino
Here we have a mix of Latin Dances where there is no need for a partner, which is interesting rather than social!

Balboa
A fast tempo dance belonging to the 'Swing' family of dances.

Beguine
The Beguine is a type of Rumba.

Black Bottom
The Black Bottom is a dance which evolved in the Charleston era of New York during the 1920s; it consists of shuffles, knee sways and stomps.

Bolero
Bolero is a slow tempo dance in 3/4 time, which originated in Spain during the 18th century. The music usually has a triplet on the second beat of each bar. One must be prepared for the unexpected pauses and sharp turns in this dance, though.

Boogie Woogie

With its roots in the Rock 'n' Roll dances of the 1950s, this is the name given to an African American jazz dance where the knees are held close together and the hips sway from side to side, during which the dancer travels forward. ('Boogie' has also become the slang word for 'dance' – 'Let's have a little boogie!')

Bosa Nova

This is one of the many dances that were either born in, or grew to prominence in the freedom of the swinging 60s, with this particular dance developing through the fusion of jazz and Brazilian music.

Boston Jive

This is a form of Swing dance, very similar to the Lindy Hop, but, in this case, with kicks added.

Bourrée

Sometimes danced in wooden clogs, this is a French Baroque dance of quick skipping steps.

Bunny Hop

This is the name given to a dance that is similar to the more well known Conga line.

Can Can

A popular, and one could even say 'famous', dance born in 19th-century France, in which the girls wear sensuous corsets and carry out, high kicking routines which are accompanied by much vocal shouting and screaming. The Cancan is now virtually a tourist attraction of Paris.

Cha Cha

Once called the Cha Cha Cha (three Chas instead of two!), this dance actually originated from the Mambo and became the triple Mambo before becoming a dance in its own right. Please note, though, that no one now seems to be able to agree on whether to call it the Cha Cha or the Cha Cha Cha, all of which makes it very confusing for the novice dancer!

Carioca
The Carioca is Brazilian dance similar to the Samba.

Charleston
The Charleston is a dance which originated during the American prohibition of the 1920s and has probably one of the most fascinating dance 'stories'. The Charleston, it is said, originated in the Speakeasies, (establishments which sold illegal liquor of the time), when the jazz music was extremely loud and the floors very slippery thus meaning that dancers had no option but to quickly flick their feet if they wanted to remain in an upright position. This movement then became characteristic of the dance which became known as the Charleston.

Conga
This is an African/Cuban dance and usually danced in a Conga chain; this is traditionally where one person stands behind another, holding on to his or her waist. The resulting long line – chain – then weaves its way around the room, even down the streets! The steps for the Conga are extremely simple and repetitive – one, two, three, kick, over and over again, with the kick often accompanied by cries of 'Hcy!' by the participants.

Continental or International Tango
This is probably the most difficult of all the 'Smooth' dances as it requires perfect control and musical phrasing. It is actually a more sophisticated and technical version of the Argentine Tango.

Contredanse
The Contredanse is an 18th century folk dance, developed by the French from traditional English folk dances, in which two lines of couples face each other – one line made up of men and the other of women.

Cotillion
Another French court dance, and a precursor to the Quadrille, this is an elaborate Ballroom Dance with frequent changes of partner – and what could be more 'social' than that!

Cotton-Eyed Joe
A very energetic, exciting and fun Country and Western dance in which the participants indulge in stomps, shuffles, kicks and turns, instead of simply travelling around the room.

Czardas
A Hungarian folk dance developed in the 19th century from an earlier folk dance, this is a dance that increases in speed and which has wonderful syncopated rhythms.

Dashing White Sergeant
A traditional 'progressive' Scottish folk dance performed by groups of six dancers. The Dashing White Sergeant was frequently learned by children in schools during the 1950s and 1960s.

Dominican Merengue
As the name would suggest, this is the dance of the Dominican Republic, where interestingly the syncopation of the first beat in the music is interpreted by the dancers as a slight limp!

Fandango
This is a name with which most of us are familiar, for surely we have all heard the saying 'doing the Fandango'. So what is it? It is the name of a Spanish dance performed with either castanets or tambourines and one which begins slowly to the sound of clicking fingers and stomping feet. The speed of the dance then gradually increases throughout, ending on a flamboyant high.

Fish
The Fish is a popular, sexually based dance, that uses the music of the Foxtrot as the dancers rock their pelvises back and forth, balancing first on one foot and then on the other.

Flamenco
The Flamenco is a gypsy dance, generally executed to guitar music, and is known for its heelwork.

Freestyle/Disco
Currently a very popular style of dance and very energetic, it involves great diversity of steps, including leaps, kicks and spins. It is a style of dance that is very popular with the young – hardly surprising when one thinks of the high energy levels required!

Gavotte
This dance originated in France during the 16th century, with one of its greatest admirers being Marie Antoinette.

Gay Gordons
Danced at ceilidhs, this is traditionally the first dance of the evening, danced in couple to music in march time and progressively around the room. Again, like the Dashing White Sergeant, this was frequently taught to schoolchildren in the 1950s and 1960s. It is also a popular hogmanay dance.

Habanera
The Habanera is a slow and seductive Cuban dance.

Hornpipe
A favourite with many children, this dance originated around 1760 and is generally known for its famous rocking movement of the ankles.

Hula
I think almost everyone knows that the origin of this dance is Hawaiian. The use of the arms, hands and facial expressions, as well as the excessive and expressive use of the swaying hips, was the reason for the missionaries to – originally – ban it!

Hustle
This is primarily a disco dance from the 1970s.

Jarabe
The Jarabe, with a rhythm resembling the Mazurka, is a typical Mexican folk dance. In America it is known as the Mexican Hat Dance.

Jig
A springy and sprightly dance – which is why we are often said to be doing a jig when we are happy or 'jigging around' when we can't keep still.

Jitterbug
The Jitterbug is a social dance that was very popular in the 1930s.

Lambada
This is a relatively new dance on the Ballroom floor and is a mixture of the Rumba and the Samba.

Lambeth Walk
Originally an old English step from the Limehouse district of London and a dance which was made famous by the musical *Me and My Girl*.

Limbo
A very difficult dance – if not impossible – for anyone who is not extremely flexible, for this involves dancing under a horizontal pole which is moved progressively lower as time goes on. It is a dance of the West Indies.

Lindy Hop
A dance which originated in the 1920s, supposedly named after Charles Lindbergh's flight to Paris in 1927, when the newspaper headline read LINDY HOPS THE ATLANTIC.

Mambo
The origin of this fast and fun filled dance is Cuba.

Marcha
This is the Latin American version of the One Step.

Matachin
The Matachin is a Spanish ritualised sword dance or battle dance.

Mazurka
This is a Polish national dance. It is a 'proud' style of dance, characterised by clicking of the heels

Mento
This is the most popular native dance of Jamaica and resembles a Rumba played in slow tempo.

Merengue
The Merengue is the Dominican Republic's own party dance. Many of the Merengue movements are similar to those of the Salsa, but with a slower tempo. It is also known as the Dominican Merengue, just in case anyone wants to lay claim to it, I suppose!

Military Two Step
This is another dance that forms part of a ceilidh evening. It is lively and bouncy in style and is danced fairly early on in the ceilidh evening.

Minuet
The Minuet was originally a peasant folk dance of Poitou, introduced in Paris in the 1650s, and is said to have dominated the Ballroom from that time until the close of the 18th century. It is an elegant dance in ¾ time, with pretty, delicate movements, as the name would imply.

Morris Dance
A centuries old folk dance often performed on village greens, in village squares and so on; it is accompanied and characterised by the wearing of bells, which jingle when the dancers move, the waving of handkerchiefs and striking of sticks, etc. It is a great tourist attraction in the typical English villages.

One Step
The One Step is made up entirely of chassés without any change in rhythm.

Passacaglia
A slow solemn Italian or Spanish dance.

Passepied
This is a Breton dance resembling a quick Minuet.

Polka
The Polka is a Bohemian folk dance that became popular in the Ballroom genre during the 19th century.

Quadrille
A Quadrille is a square dance for four couples.

Reel
A much loved and popular, lively dance of the Scottish Highlands.

Rock 'n' Roll
The dance of youth, this is a popular form of the Swing or Lindy Hop.

Schottische
This is a Scottish dance, which is in fact a lot like a Polka.

Shag
A hopping Ballroom dance from the 1930s.

Shimmy
Originally a dance in its own right, this has now become the description for the move itself which characterised the dance and that is the shoulder and body shaking 'shimmy'.

Square Dance
An American folk dance consisting of an even number of couples who form a square, two lines, or a circle. A caller then instructs the dancers on what movements are required.

Stomp
A Jazz dance that involves a lot of foot stamping or stomping.

Swing
This is a mix of various African American dances which has evolved into the Ballroom and nightclub versions of today. It is based on two slow and two quick counts.

Tango
A social dance which, although originating in Spain, actually developed in Argentina under the influence of the rhythm of black dance styles. There are essentially three types of Tango: the Argentine, the American and the International.

Tarantella
Sounds a bit like a scary spider but is in fact a dance originating in Italy, in which one dancer turns or spins in place before being joined, after a while, by their partner.

Turkey Trot
A dance to fast ragtime music with the basic steps consisting of four hopping steps sideways on one leg and then repeated on the other. Scissor-like flicks of the feet and fast trotting actions with abrupt stops are then added.

Twist
A dance made popular in, and a huge part of, the 1960s culture, this was actually created in the late 1950s, but really only 'took off', as they say, in 1960 when Chubby Checker – a name that was set to become synonymous with the dance and the word Twist – made his first 'Twist' recording.

Two Step
This is a simple dance that actually is more or less a double quick march. It has a skip in each step and is executed as fast as a couple can dance!

Veleta
An English Ballroom, Sequence dance for couples with ladies standing on the outside and the gentlemen on the inside

Volte
A predecessor of the Waltz, where the man turns his partner around several times and then assists her as she takes a high spring into the air.

Zamacueca
The Zamacueca is a Chilean dance where partners move around each other.

Ziganka
A Russian country dance.

Zoppetto
A medieval Italian limping, hop dance.

SEQUENCE DANCING

To the outsider this seems a rather complex member of the Ballroom Dancing world, and so to simplify it, let's start at the beginning by attempting to answer the obvious question: what is Sequence Dancing? Well, basically a Sequence Dance is where all dancers on the dance floor dance the same 16 bar prearranged sequence of steps, (although the number of bars can vary, 16 is the most common), together and all at the same time too, each sequence having its own name to ensure uniformity from Lands End to John O'Groats. It might seem a little bizarre to those not familiar with this style of dance, but I think that there is something quite comforting about Sequence Dancing, where everyone is doing the same thing at the same time and in the same place. It must be the feeling of camaraderie that it gives out! Perhaps, then, it is as a consequence of this camaraderie feel that Sequence Dancing does have a good and loyal following at the various clubs dedicated to such throughout the UK.

The steps for the scripted dances are probably easier to learn as opposed to those required for single pair dancing. This is possibly because the set figures continually repeat themselves to the chosen number of bars of music – be they eight, sixteen or thirty two bars – which, I suppose, also brings a security net into the equation. So, to summarise, Sequence Dancing equals: repetition, security and camaraderie.

Now Sequence Dancing can in general be divided into three main sections those section being: Classical Sequence, Modern Sequence and Latin Sequence. The Classical section covers what used to be known as 'Old Time Dancing.' The name was actually changed from Old Time to Classical as it was thought that 'old' would deter people from taking up this style of dance, a style which included dances such as the Old Time Waltz, Gavottes and Two Steps. (Here I must mention, to avoid confusion, that there are three types of Waltz: the original Old Time Waltz, based on the five balletic foot positions; the rather slower Modern Waltz, with parallel foot technique; and the Viennese Waltz, also using parallel footwork, but at a much faster speed.) Such dances as these were at the height of their popularity before the First World War, although they did enjoy a revival after the Second World War and through to the late 1950s. I for one can clearly remember doing the Military Two Step and the Veleta at the afternoon tea dances which I went to with my mother in the North Eastern seaside resort of Scarborough, back in the 1950s. I was eleven years old at the time. Now how uncool would that be today, but what fun it was then! As one would expect, the Modern Sequence Dances comprise of the Quickstep, Waltz, Foxtrot and Tango, just as in Ballroom Dancing which itself is rising in popularity thanks to the phenoneman that is *Strictly Come Dancing*. Many of the same steps are used in the scripted sequences for this section as in the pair dances of Ballroom Dancing. Following in the same vein then Latin Sequence Dances draw their steps from the standard Latin American Dances such as the Cha Cha, Rumba, Paso Doble and so on.

Generally speaking, this style of dancing actually evolved from many of the European country dances which date back to as early as the 10th century and which were then passed down through the centuries from village to village, town to town, from one generation to the next and so on, being altered/refined along the way, until finally reaching ... well, us really! It is thought, however, that the more immediate parentage of Sequence Dancing can be found in the 17th century courts of France and England, whereafter it continued to grow in popularity until the early part of the 1900s, when the Old Time Dances developed to include Gavottes, Mazurkas and Quick Waltzes (the latter became the Viennese Waltz, which was taken over by the Modern Ballroom Dancers). These were then followed by Two Steps (martial music), Saunters (a Foxtrot-type of dance but much slower), Swings (Ragtime and Quickstep based) and Tangos, so making up the traditional Old Time dance form. Sadly now, though, such dances from the Old Time (Classical) dance era such as the Military Two Step and the Veleta are not as popular as they were at the beginning of the 20th century, though having said that there are a number of Sequence clubs that dedicate themselves solely – or at least mainly – to the Old Time (Classical) Sequences Dances. And whilst some could be forgiven for thinking that this is a style of dance which is out-moded and in danger of extinction, they certainly need to think again, for there are, in fact, followers and clubs on an International basis where enthusiasts regularly meet, sometimes several times a week, to enjoy their particular favourite style of Sequence Dancing. An interesting fact to note is that Old Time Sequence clubs can be found in at least 15 countries globally and would appear to be more popular than the Modern Ballroom Sequence or Latin American Sequence.

Now, on to the dances themselves, of which there are literally thousands in all of the three sections. I cannot, of course, include all of them, or in fact very many of them at all to be honest, and so instead you will find below just a few to whet your appetite. I must own up here, though, to being a little self-indulgent at this stage, for I have actually included the Military Two Step in this section, which is apparently danced very rarely these days. However, as, along with the Veleta, this was the dance that my mother and I enjoyed most, and so I have included it is as a tribute to her – maybe with the bonus being that some of you may try them out and add them to your programmes once more!

Balmoral Blues
Here we have a sequence slow Foxtrot dance, danced with parallel feet.

Boston Two Step
This Old Time Sequence Dance is a march and is danced with turned-out feet.

Circassian Circle
Although not as well known as many of the other dances I have included this one because it is fun, easy to learn and as a progressive dance encourages the more shy participants to mix, which is always a recipe for success at any dance. Generally danced to a reel, it can also be danced to a jig.

Dashing White Sergeant
Frequently danced at Scottish ceilidhs and at primary schools as an introduction to the joys of dancing. It is more energetic than the Gay Gordons but no more difficult and lots of fun.

Emmerdale Waltz

A modern Waltz with some old time elements; for example the solo turns and the hover, and whisk in double hold.

Eva Three Step

This is a stately and popular dance in 4/4 time, originally a Gavotte, but nowadays danced in two-step timing. It is called a three step because in all first four bars there are three steps and point.

Harry Lime Foxtrot

This dance is actually more of a Saunter than a Slow Foxtrot with its walks, chassés, points and twinkles. In its simplicity it is an easy dance to both perform and remember.

Lilac Waltz

Exactly as the name implies, this is a Waltz and, as an Old Time Waltz, there are relatively few dancing figures but there are a lot of movements involving the arms, feet and head.

Mayfair Quickstep

An Old Time Sequence Quickstep danced with parallel feet and generally in progressive fashion. It has many Old Time features and could well be called a Swing. The Ballroom hold is not maintained at all times as the dance starts and finishes in open hold and incorporates solo turns for both the gentleman and the lady.

Military Two Step

A lively dance to march music, concluding with an eight bar Waltz sequence.

Pride of Erin Waltz

A non progressive Sequence Waltz danced to Old Time music.

Quadrilles and Lancers

The historic dances performed by four couples in a square.

Royal Empress Tango
This dance shares several of the dancing figures with the Saunters and can even be danced to the music used for a Saunter.

Regis Waltz
The Regis Waltz is an Old Time Waltz based on the balletic foot position

Sindy Swing
This is a very popular Sequence Dace for, as well as being a recent addition to the 'Sequence' family, it is a favourite with both Modern and Old Time Sequence Dancers and is generally danced in the progressive fashion.

Square Tango
The Square Tango is danced in Ballroom hold throughout which though this would generally imply it is a Modern Sequence dance it is actually classed as a Classical Sequence dance.

Square Tango 2
Lots of repetition in this dance makes it fairly straightforward and so relatively easy – even for the novice.

Veleta
Another Old Time Waltz in the Sequence family of dances.

Tango Serida
An Old Time Dance which, just like the Waverley, has been a medalist and competition dance for many years.

Waltz Marie
This is said to be one of the most popular Sequence Dances of all time, even to the point that it actually has many regional variations.

Waverley Two Step
A dance, which is popular with the Old Time social dancers, the Waverley is a medalist and competition dance.

DANCE TERMS AND DEFINITIONS

In all of my books I have made a point of including the terms and definitions peculiar to the subject in question, and it is no different in this book. However, I do believe that in the arts there are often no definitive boundaries, with each genre borrowing a little from other genres, which in turn appear under the larger umbrella of art in general and more specifically, in this case, of dance. I figure that if you are interested in dance, then it is probably an interest as a whole, although you may in part prefer one particular form to another, be it Ballet or Ballroom Dancing, for example. Of course, one must always remember that Ballet is the stabilising core of all dance and so to understand basic balletic terms is essential if you are interested in any form of dance. And so the following terms cross the fluid boundaries of dance, being dance specific rather than genre specific.

A

action
Latin American Dancing is all about 'hip action', which is directly related to the use of feet on the floor, for if the weight is taken through the ball of the foot, through to the heel, the leg then straightens and the hip follows through.

adagio
Any dance executed to slow music is called an adagio; it is also a part of the classical pas de deux in Ballet.

air, en l'
Translated, this means 'in the air' and indicates that the movement in question should actually be made 'in the air'.

alegrias
Usually danced by a woman alone, this is a Spanish gypsy dance and suggests the movements of a bullfight.

alignment
This refers to the direction of the feet in relation to the line of the dance.

allegro
A term which tells the dancer that all the movements should be brisk, happy and lively.

allongé
A term used in Ballet to describe an elongated line, especially the horizontal line of an arabesque, where one arm is stretched out to the front and the other out to the back.

amalgamation
This term describes a combination of two or more dance patterns or movements.

American spin
This is when the gentleman lets go of the lady and lets her spin on her own.

anchor
The 'anchor' is the finale rhythm in a Swing dance and so dictates in which position the dancers will end.

appel
This is preparation step used in the Paso Doble and is a stamping action before a movement.

arabesque
A position that involves the dancer standing on one leg, straight or bent, with the other extended to the back at a 90° angle.

arrastre
Here we have the term for a drag.

arrière, en
This tells you that the step is taken in a backward direction whilst moving away from the audience.

assemblé
This is the term used to describe a jump from one foot to both feet, and then usually landing in fifth position.

attitude
Generally this is a word used to describe a rebellious teenager! However, in the world of dance, attitude is used to describe a pose in which one leg is raised to the back or to the front with knee bent and usually with arm raised.

avant en
This tells you that the step is taken forward and toward the audience.

axel turn
An axel turn is basically two turns in one.

B

baion
This is a type of slow Samba rhythm which originated in Brazil and became popular in North America in the 1950s.

balancé
Translated, this means 'to swing' or 'to rock', and is a term used to describe a step where the dancer rocks from one foot to the other.

balançoire
This is when a grand battement is executed with a continuous swinging motion through the first position to the fourth position, front and back.

ball change
This is a very basic dance step learned early on in training, even by the youngest of dancers, and means the transference of weight from the ball of one foot to the flat of the other foot.

ballon
This is the ability of a dancer to remain suspended mid-air during the execution of a jump.

barrida
The term used to describe a sweep.

bas, en
A term used to indicate a low position of the arms.

basque, pas de
This is a movement which is halfway between a step and a leap.

battement
This term is used to describe the beating movement of the legs.

battu
Any step that has been embellished with a beat is called a battu.

botafogo
Botafogo is a travelling walk with a change of direction from left to right or from right to left.

bourrée, pas de
This is a series of small, fast steps which are executed with the feet very close together. It is a simple connecting step used to link other steps in a combination.

bras
In classical dance this is the name for arms and nothing to do with underwear

break
In dance, this means to change direction.

break step
The term used for a two step sequence in Latin Dances which changes the direction of movement and where the first and second steps are taken in opposition.

brisé
A brisé is a small beating step in which the movement is broken.

C

cabriole
An elevated step in which the extended legs are beaten in the air. The working leg is thrust into the air whilst the underneath leg follows and beats against the first leg, sending it higher, before the dancer lands on the underneath leg.

catch step
This is a flat-footed ball change.

centre
Balance point of the body mass; it is situated near the diaphragm.

chaînés
This is a series of rapid turns on half or full pointe with the legs in first position, rotating a half turn on one foot and the other half turn on the other foot. They are executed one after the other, so they are in effect 'chained' together.

change step
A step used to help dancers move from one foot to the other in between the natural and reverse steps.

changement
This is a jump that starts in fifth position with one foot in front and landing in fifth position with the alternate foot in front.

chassé
This term describes a sliding step where one foot chasés and then displaces the other foot. The chassé can travel in any direction, including rotation. It is a basic step used in the Cha Cha and Jive, where it consists of three steps: side close side; forward cross forward; back cross back.

chat, pas de
Meaning 'step of the cat', this is a cat-like leap in which one foot follows the other into the air, during which the knees are bent and after which the landing is in the fifth position.

checked forward walk
Sounds a bit like a walking table cloth, but it actually means to take a step forward and then immediately change direction.

ciseaux
This word describes a scissor-like jump.

close hold
This is the normal hold for most Ballroom Dances and is when the partners' bodies are close together.

coaster step
The pattern of this step is back – together – forward, and it is a triple step often used in Swing dancing.

combination
In the dance world, the word combination is used to describe a series of steps which are linked together.

compensating step
The term given to a step which gels together two different rhythms.

contra body movement (CBM)
In this movement the torso, with the shoulders and hips aligned, twist one way from the legs; opposition of the leading foot to the opposite shoulder.

contra body movement position (CBMP)
This is the placing of the foot – forward or back – on to or across the line of the other foot, thus giving the false appearance of a contra body movement being used.

coupé
Meaning to cut, this describes a small intermediary step taken in preparation for another step, when the foot is pulled sharply off the floor and then placed either in front or back of the ankle.

Cuban motion
A term used to describe a discreet, though sensuous, hip movement.

cucarachas
An interesting word which literally means 'crushing beetles'. (Did a dancer stand on the beetle, then?) For this step, which is used in Latin American Dancing, the dancers start with their feet together before one foot steps to the side, (to crush the 'mythical' beetle) before closing back to its original position. An alternative and easier to remember name for this is – 'side breaks' – which actually is not nearly as impressive when you are a small child, or novice for that matter, and showing off your knowledge!

D

dancesport
This is what competitive Ballroom Dancing is now called.

déboulés
A series of half turns executed alternately on each foot.

demi-plié
All steps of elevation begin and end with a demi-plié, which is a half-bend of the knees.

derrière
This means behind the body and generally indicates that the working foot is closed at the back.

devant
This means in front of the body.

developpé
A word which, in the dance world, means unfolding the leg in mid air.

dig swivel
A foot dig that is then followed by a swivel on the balls of the feet.

double hand hold
A hold in which the dance partners stand opposite each other and hold hands. It is adopted when the partners wish to practise the steps before taking the relevant and correct open or close hold.

drop
A simple word used to describe a movement where the weight of one of the dance partners is either partially or completely supported by the other, while at least one part of the body remains in contact with the floor.

E
écarté
This term describes the extension of one leg at an oblique angle – the body too is at an oblique angle during the execution of the move.

elevation
This is a jump by the dancer, which gives the impression of suspension at the apex.

enrosque
A term meaning a twist.

entrechat
A Ballet term to describe a dancer repeatedly crossing his or her legs in mid air.

épaulement
This term is used to describe the position of the body, but only from the waist up.

F
fado
This was originally a Portuguese song and dance but is now a term used in the Samba with the steps based on a hop, a skip and a kick.

fallaway
In a fallaway the couple is in promenade position, but travelling backwards.

fan
A fan is a position where the gentleman and lady are at right angles to each other. It is a position used in both the Rumba and the Cha-Cha.

feather step
When the gentleman steps outside of the lady it is called a feather step.

fermé
The word used to describe the feet in a closed position.

figure
Figure refers to a series of steps linked together as a unit.

figure eight
This term is a description of the hips when they roll around in the figure of eight.

five positions
The five basic positioned placings of the feet in the art of dancing, which were originally set by the dancing master Pierre Beauchamp in the late 17th century, are as follows:

First Position: This is when the feet are in a straight line with the heels touching.

Second Position: In this position the legs and heels are apart – by about the length of one's foot – with the toes turned out at 180 degrees, or slightly less.

Third Position: This is when the feet are turned out – one foot in front of the other foot – with the heel of the front foot in the hollow of the instep of the back foot.

Fourth Position: In this position the feet – separated by about the length of one's foot – are apart and turned out.

Fifth Position: This is similar to third position but with the heel of the front foot touching the base of the big toe of the rear foot.

flex
To bend or relax a specific part of the body.

flick
For want of a better word, this is a kick from the knee.

follow through
A term used when the non-supporting foot passes by the weighted foot before it changes direction.

fondu
Food springs to mind here, but in dance it is a term used to describe the lowering of the body by the bending of the knee.

footwork
When we talk of footwork, we are referring to the part of the foot/feet that is/are in contact with the dance floor during the execution of a step.

forward walk turning
A Latin American term used in the Rumba and Cha Cha and which means to step forward but end backwards, for example as in the fan and the hockey stick.

fouette
This is when a dancer's leg 'whips' out and then returns to the knee as the dancer turns on the supporting leg, rising on to pointe.

freestyle
This is just as the name implies – free – that is, the style of the dance is neither restricted nor governed by rules or conventions.

G
glissade
A sliding step that connects two other steps.

grand battement
This is a controlled leg lift in which the working leg is 'thrown' as high as possible whilst keeping the rest of the body aligned.

grand jeté
A big leap forward (see 'jeté').

grapevine
The pattern of a grapevine is made through perfectly executed footwork in a continuous travelling step, pattern, to the side as the trailing foot alternately crosses behind and/or in front.

H

hitch kick
For this the dancer gives a little jump up, with one knee in the air, and as soon as he/she hits the ground then the other leg goes into a high kick, the former move being a preparation for the second and much higher kick.

hockey stick
This is a move in the Rumba and Cha-Cha, so called because the lady's moves form a pattern similar to those made by an ice or field hockey stick.

hoofer
In the 1920s this term was used to describe any dancer, though it later became the name by which only tap dancers were known.

I

in line
To step between your partner's feet.

inside turn
A dance movement that requires the lady to turn to her left, under the man's left hand, or to her right, under the man's right hand.

isolation
This is when one part of a dancer's body moves independently to the rest of the body.

J

jeté
A jeté is a leap from one leg to another.

K

kaholo
Kaholo is the name of a hula dance step.

kick
A kick generally comes from the hip.

kick ball change
A very basic dance step with which even children and beginners soon become familiar and which is made up of a sequence of three steps consisting of kicks, a step on the ball of the foot followed by another step on the opposite foot.

L

Latin American dances
There are two divisions of Latin dances; these are the traditional dances and then there are the standard non-Hispanic dances, such as the Bolero, Cha Cha, Mambo, Paso Doble, Rumba and Samba.

Latin cross
A term that means to chassé forwards or backwards with the feet crossing on the middle step.

leading
One partner, when a couple dance together, leads – is leading – the other in terms of direction and movements etc. This is generally the man, when the couple is made up of a man and a woman, but when two women dance together it is usually the better and more confident of the two, and sometimes simply the taller.

lean
A movement where one partner leans into or away from the other partner, and where the non-leaning partner supports the one leaning.

leads
In Latin American Dancing the gentleman can lead the lady by means of a physical lead through his hands and arms or by a shaping lead through the shape of his body.

leaverage move
A move of counterbalance where one partner counterbalances the other in order to prevent a fall.

line
The aesthetic extension of the body, including the arms and legs.

line of dance (LOD)
For Modern Ballroom Dances and Latin American Dances, this represents an imaginary line drawn anti-clockwise around the dance floor – with the outer wall of the room you are in being the equivalent of the pavement and the buildings. As a general note just imagine the chaos if there were no rules governing the trafficking of dancers in a Ballroom! So to ensure safety and comfort of all, progression around the dance floor is always anti-clockwise, (wall to the right of the dancers, centre to the left).

lunge
A leg bent forward takes the weight as the other leg is extended behind.

M

merengue
As well as being an actual Latin American dance, merengue is also a term used to refer to hip action.

muso
The shortened – and more affectionate – term given to the word musician, it is used throughout the entertainment world and not just the dance world.

N

natural turn
A turn in which the partners turn around each other clockwise.

O

open break

This is a break step taken in open facing position and usually with the partners dancing in opposition, meaning in fact that they both break back simultaneously.

open hold

Generally used in the Latin Dances when the dancers' bodies are slightly apart.

opposition

A movement or position of the arms in the opposite direction to the movement or position of the legs – opposing limb movement.

outside partner

This means to step to the side of your partner's feet, and not in line.

outside turn

Here is a turn in which the lady turns to her right under the man's left hand or she turns to her left and so under the man's right hand.

P

paddle turn

A turn either to the left or to the right, using a series of ball changes with three quarters of the weight staying over the turning foot.

pas

Literally translated, this means movement or step.

pas de deux

A dance for two, usually a gentleman and a lady.

passé

Here we have a movement in which the pointed foot of the working leg is made to pass the knee of the supporting leg.

patada
This is the term used to describe a kick.

penché
A penché is an extreme arabesque in which the body stays lifted and extended, tilting towards the floor whilst keeping the back straight as the back leg goes up and out as far as possible and with the arms extended to almost touch the floor.

pirouette
This is the term used for a complete 180° turn of the body and which is performed on one leg.

pivot turn
A 180° turn on the ball of one foot, performed in extended third foot position with the thighs locked. A series of pivot turns creates travelling rotations, with 180° of rotation per weight change.

plié
This is the term for the bending of the knees, which is executed in any of the five basic foot positions. (A demi-plié is a half-bending of the knees where the heels are on the floor and a grand-plié is a full bending of the knees.)

pointe
This means the tip of the toe. A dancer dances en pointes in special shoes called pointe shoes.

port de bras
This is the term used when describing the position of the arms in Ballet.

practice hold
A hold adopted when dance partners wish to practise the steps before taking the relevant and correct open or close hold. It is also known as a double hand hold.

prep
Short for 'preparation' this is a lead-in movement or a step used as a preparation for a turn or a change of dance position.

promenade position (pp)
In Ballroom Dancing this is when the man's right side and the lady's left side are in contact at the ribcage level, with the opposite sides of the body turned out to form a V. In Latin American dancing it is exactly the same apart from the fact that the bodies do not touch with the only point of contact being the hands.

Q

quick
This has nothing to do with the speed of a dance but actually describes a step or weight change that takes one beat of music.

R

release
The 'letting go' of whatever forced movement or pose your body was in at the time.

relevé
Translated from the French, this means lifted or raised and is when the heels are lifted or raised off the floor, with or without the help of a plié, up on to pointe or demi-pointe.

retiré
A position in which the working foot is drawn up to the knee of the supporting leg.

reverence
A bow or curtsey taken in Ballet.

reverse turn
This turn is the near-mirror counterpart of the natural turn, turning counter-clockwise.

ride
During the execution of this movement one partner supports and rotates the other partner; it is sometimes known as 'the horse and cart'.

rise and fall
A term frequently used in the world of Ballroom Dancing which is exactly as the words imply, and that is the controlled rise and fall of the body during the dance sequence; it is most obvious in the Waltz and adds to the graceful feel of the dance.

roll
When the two dancers' bodies are brought closer together in a rotating motion.

rond de jambe
A term meaning 'circle of the leg'.

rosin
A substance used by dancers on the soles of their shoes to prevent them from slipping.

S

sacada
A term meaning the displacement of feet.

sailor step
A triple step which is executed by leaning in the other direction of a crossed foot.

Samba bounce action
This is caused by the bending and straightening of the knees.

shoulder leads
This is when a dancer takes a step with the same shoulder leading as the foot.

salida
A term for a basic walking pattern within a dance sequence.

Samba roll
This means a rolling movement from the waist up.

shadow position
A term used to describe a position where the lady is placed in front of the gentleman or vice versa.

shimmy
When a dancer shakes his/her shoulders or entire body, then he is said to be doing a shimmy, or shimmying.

shine
This is the section in a Latin Dance where the partners break free from each other and do their own thing, thus allowing them to 'shine'.

side by side
A term to describe a dance position in which both dancers are facing the same way.

slash
Also known as the slide movement, this is when one partner transports the other partner, who at all times maintains contact with the floor.

snake
The snake is an 'S' movement starting from the head and curving the body sideways in slinky movement all the way through the body, going to the other side in a seamlessly, effortless manner.

solo position
This is a term used when the dancing partners make no contact with each other.

spin turn
This turn has a pivoting action for the gentleman and a brushing action for the lady. The movement begins with the first three steps of a natural turn.

spotting
A dancer is said to be spotting when he/she fixes his/her eyes on one spot while turning several times in quick succession during a dance sequence; doing this helps the dancer to not feel dizzy, whilst thus keeping their balance.

step
The movement of the foot from one position to the next.

syncopation
In the dancing world this has come to mean the splitting of a beat into two parts. (Musicians would say that this is shifting the accent from a stronger beat to a weaker one, thus creating a different rhythm.)

sway
This is the inclination of the body to the right or to the left and gives the lilting movement of the body, especially in the Waltz. It is never used in the Tango.

T

terre à terre
A term used to describe steps in which the dancer's feet do not leave the floor.

tour en l'air
A turn in the air as the dancer jumps with the body held vertically straight.

tour jeté
A jump from one foot to the other whilst performing a half turn.

turnout
This is a dancer's ability to turn his or her feet and upper legs, (thighs), out from the hip joints up to a position of 90°. A good turnout is particularly useful in the Latin American Dances.

twinkles
A lovely, quaint term found in the Sequence Dance world, where quick and slow twinkles are the standard figures used in marching in order to change the leading foot to get into step.

V

volé, de
Used to describe a step executed with a flying or soaring movement.

volta
This means crossing over of the feet. These steps can also be done on the spot, when they are called 'Spot Voltas'.

W

whisk
A popular dance figure which was first created in the Waltz around the 1930s.

weave
This is a step all on the toes – though not high on toes.

working leg
This means the leg that is executing the given movement whilst the weight of the body is on the other leg.

TANGO TERMINOLOGY

More for fun than anything else, here are a few terms pertinent to the Tango.

abrazo
the embrace

adornos
embellishments

arrastre
a drag

bailar
this means to dance

barrida
this is when the foot of one partner sweeps the foot of the other partner

boleo
this is used to describe the quick flick of the lower leg

caminar
the basic walking pattern of the Tango

corte
a cut

corrida
double-time walking, a rhythmic run

cruzada
to cross

enrosque
a twist

gancho
hook

giro
turn

golpecitos
this means little toe taps

golpes
toe taps

milonguero
a frequent dancer

ocho
a figure eight

sacada
a displacement

sentada
sitting move

tanda
this is a set of dance music and generally consists of three to five songs

tanguera
the word for a female dancer

tanguero
the word for a male dancer

rulo
curl

Vals
an Argentine Waltz

volcada
a word meaning a falling step

HONOURING THE CHAMPIONS

Ballroom Dancing has, since the year 2004, enjoyed a huge surge in popularity, thanks in the main to the TV programme *Strictly Come Dancing* and as a result is no longer considered as 'the old fogies pastime' but instead is considered a rather cool way to spend leisure time for all ages. Ballroom Dancing has now been finally recognised as a bone fide sport too, which is as exactly as it should be, for no other sporting activity has been as successful as Ballroom Dancing in winning championships for Great Britain, a fact highlighted in 1992 when Queen Elizabeth II held a garden party to celebrate the 40th anniversary of her accession to the throne, to which she invited all of the sportsmen and sportswomen who, during her 40 years reign, had won a World Championship for Britain. And guess what? On that day no less than 55 British Ballroom World Dance Champions were at the Palace. You see we not only 'rule the waves', but we clearly 'rule the dance floor' as well! Sadly however, it is a little-known fact just how successful we are as a nation in the Ballroom Dance world. I can't understand why though when there is so much evidence out there just staring us all in the face.

There are, in fact, competitive dance couples who have received the MBE (Member of the British Empire) from The Queen in recognition of their achievements in competitive dancing. Those recipients are:

Marcus and Karen Hilton
Donnie Burns and Gaynor Fairweather
Bill and Bobbie Irvine
Frank and Peggy Spencer
Stephen Hillier

WORLD CHAMPIONS

In an age where competition is often frowned upon and everyone is considered a winner for just taking part, it is actually good to see a table of champions. A friend of mine – who I hasten to add is very competitive – once told me that if you come second in any competition then, contrary to fashionable beliefs, you have not done well and are in fact a loser. He believes that there is only one place to come in a competition and that is first. As old fashioned as it is, I agree with this! What is the point of taking part if you are happy to lose? How satisfying then must it be to be a 'World Champion', as some of the following have been declared?

It was in Paris in the year 1909 that the first World Championship in Ballroom Dancing was held, although accurate records of these early events are hard to come by. In 1922 the sport was split into amateur and professional levels and from then on records were kept and so we can look back with pride and see that in this sport the UK dominates the world.

We will start then with those who have been recognised as world champions in the field of Ballroom Dancing. Please note though that these following details are from the dates the competitions were officially recognised, and I do apologise to anyone I may have inadvertently omitted from any of the lists on the following pages.

BACKBEND – A move for the experienced and competitive dancer – don't try this one at home! (Reproduced with kind permission of the artist Stephanie Jones)

BALLROOM DANCE WORLD CHAMPIONS

YEAR	MALE PARTNER	FEMALE PARTNER	COUNTRY
1922	Victor Silvester	Phyllis Clark	Endland
1923	Maxwell Stewart	Barbara Miles	England
1924	Maxwell Stewart	Barbara Miles	England
1925	Henry Catalan		Spain
1926	Maxwell Stewart	Pat Sykes	England
1927	Edward Blunt	Doris Germai	England
1928	Maxwell Stewart	Pat Sykes	England
1929	Herbert Jemull	Gerti Hepprich	England
1930	Maxwell Stewart	Pat Sykes	England
1931	Arthur Milner	Norma Cave	England
1932	Marcel	Mme Chapoul	France
1933	Sydney Stern	Mae Walmsley	England
1934	Marcel	Mme Chapoul	France
1935	Marcel	Mme Chapoul	France
1936	Marcel	Mme Chapoul	France
1937	Arthur Norton	Pat Eaton	England
1938	Arthur Norton	Pat Eaton	England
1939	Arthur Norton	Pat Eaton	England
1940–1946: no competitions held during this period			
1947	Victor Barrett	Doreen Freeman	England
1948	Bob Henderson	Eileen Henshall	England
1949	Bob Henderson	Eileen Henshall	England
1950	Bob Henderson	Eileen Henshall	England
1951–1958: no competitions held during this period			
1959	Desmond Ellison	Brenda Winslade	England
1960	Bill Irvine	Bobbie Irvine	Scotland
1961	Harry Smith-Hampshire	Doreen Casey	England
1962	Bill Irvine	Bobbie Irvine	Scotland
1963	Bill Irvine	Bobbie Irvine	Scotland
1964	Bill Irvine	Bobbie Irvine	Scotland
1965	Bill Irvine	Bobbie Irvine	Scotland
1966	Peter Eggleton	Brenda Winslade	England
1967	Bill Irvine	Bobbie Irvine	Scotland
1968	Bill Irvine	Bobbie Irvine	Scotland
1969	Peter Eggleton	Brenda Winslade	England
1970	Peter Eggleton	Brenda Winslade	England

1971	Anthony Hurley	Fay Saxton	England
1972	Anthony Hurley	Fay Saxton	England
1973	Richard Gleave	Janet Gleave	England
1974	Richard Gleave	Janet Gleave	England
1975	Richard Gleave	Janet Gleave	England
1976	Richard Gleave	Janet Gleave	England
1977	Richard Gleave	Janet Gleave	England
1978	Richard Gleave	Janet Gleave	England
1979	Richard Gleave	Janet Gleave	England
1980	Richard Gleave	Janet Gleave	England
1981	Michael Barr	Vicky Barr	England
1982	Michael Barr	Vicky Barr	England
1983	Michael Barr	Vicky Barr	England
1984	Michael Barr	Vicky Barr	England
1985	Michael Barr	Vicky Barr	England
1986	Stephen Hillier	Lindsey Hillier	England
1987	Stephen Hillier	Lindsey Hillier	England
1988	Stephen Hillier	Lindsey Hillier	England
1989	John Wood	Anne Lewis	England
1990	Marcus Hilton	Karen Hilton	England
1991	Marcus Hilton	Karen Hilton	England
1992	Marcus Hilton	Karen Hilton	England
1993	Marcus Hilton	Karen Hilton	England
1994	Marcus Hilton	Karen Hilton	England
1995	Marcus Hilton	Karen Hilton	England
1996	Marcus Hilton	Karen Hilton	England
1997	Marcus Hilton	Karen Hilton	England
1998	Marcus Hilton	Karen Hilton	England
1999	Luca Baricchi	Loraine Baricchi	England
2000	Augusto Schiavo	Caterina Arzenton	Italy
2001	Luca Baricchi	Loraine Baricchi	England
2002	Christopher Hawkins	Hazel Newberry	England
2003	Christopher Hawkins	Hazel Newberry	England
2004	Christopher Hawkins	Hazel Newberry	England
2005	Mirko Gozzoli	Alessia Betti	Italy
2006	Mirko Gozzoli	Alessia Betti	Italy
2007	Mirko Gozzoli	Alessia Betti	Italy
2008	Mirko Gozzoli	Alessia Betti	Italy
2009	Arunas Bizokas	Katusha Demidova	USA

And now we will look at those who have been recognised as World Champions in the field of Latin American Dancing. Again, please note that these following details are from the dates the competitions were officially recognised.

LATIN AMERICAN DANCE WORLD CHAMPIONS

YEAR	MALE PARTNER	FEMALE PARTNER	COUNTRY
1959	Leonard Patrick	Doreen Key	England
1960	Bill Irvine	Bobbie Irvine	Scotland
1961	Bill Irvine	Bobbie Irvine	Scotland
1962	Walter Laird	Lorraine Rohdin	England
1963	Walter Laird	Lorraine Rohdin	England
1964	Walter Laird	Lorraine Rohdin	England
1965	Walter Kaiser	Marianne Kaiser	Switzerland
1966	Bill Irvine	Bobbie Irvine	Scotland
1967	Rudolph Trautz	Mechthild Trautz	Germany
1968	Bill Irvine	Bobbie Irvine	Scotland
1969	Rudolph Trautz	Mechthild Trautz	Germany
1970	Rudolph Trautz	Mechthild Trautz	Germany
1971	Rudolph Trautz	Mechthild Trautz	Germany
1972	Wolfgang Opitz	Evelyn Opitz	Germany
1973	Hans-Peter Fischer	Ingeborg Fischer	Austria
1974	Hans-Peter Fischer	Ingeborg Fischer	Austria
1975	Hans-Peter Fischer	Ingeborg Fischer	Austria
1976	Peter Maxwell	Lynn Harman	England
1977	Alan Fletcher	Hazel Fletcher	England
1978	Alan Fletcher	Hazel Fletcher	England
1979	Alan Fletcher	Hazel Fletcher	England
1980	Alan Fletcher	Hazel Fletcher	England
1981	Alan Fletcher	Hazel Fletcher	England
1982	Epsen Salberg	Kirsten Salberg	Norway
1983	Epsen Salberg	Kirsten Salberg	Norway
1984	Donnie Burns	Gaynor Fairweather	Scotland/England
1985	Donnie Burns	Gaynor Fairweather	Scotland/England
1986	Donnie Burns	Gaynor Fairweather	Scotland/England
1987	Donnie Burns	Gaynor Fairweather	Scotland/England

YEAR	MALE PARTNER	FEMALE PARTNER	COUNTRY
1988	Donnie Burns	Gaynor Fairweather	Scotland/England
1989	Donnie Burns	Gaynor Fairweather	Scotland/England
1990	Donnie Burns	Gaynor Fairweather	Scotland/England
1991	Donnie Burns	Gaynor Fairweather	Scotland/England
1992	Donnie Burns	Gaynor Fairweather	Scotland/England
1993	Donnie Burns	Gaynor Fairweather	Scotland/England
1994	Donnie Burns	Gaynor Fairweather	Scotland/England
1995	Donnie Burns	Gaynor Fairweather	Scotland/England
1996	Donnie Burns	Gaynor Fairweather	Scotland/England
1997	Hans-Reinhard Galke	Bianca Schreiber	Germany
1998	Donnie Burns	Gaynor Fairweather	Scotland/England
1999	Bryan Watson	Carmen Vincelj	Germany
2000	Bryan Watson	Carmen Vincelj	Germany
2001	Bryan Watson	Carmen Vincelj	Germany
2002	Bryan Watson	Carmen Vincelj	Germany
2003	Bryan Watson	Carmen Vincelj	Germany
2004	Bryan Watson	Carmen Vincelj	Germany
2005	Bryan Watson	Carmen Vincelj	Germany
2006	Bryan Watson	Carmen Vincelj	Germany
2007	Bryan Watson	Carmen Vincelj	Germany
2008	Michal Malitowski	Joanna Leunis	Poland
2009	Michal Malitowski	Joanna Leunis	Poland

The next World Championship is:

WORLD TEN DANCE CHAMPIONS

Now this is a confusing title for those not directly involved in the world of dance, so to explain it is a championship for couples who dance, as the title would suggest, ten dances, these being the five International Ballroom (Standard) Dances – Waltz, Foxtrot, Quickstep, Tango and Viennese Waltz, as well the five International Latin Dances – Rumba, Samba, Paso Doble, Cha-Cha-Cha and Jive.

YEAR	MALE PARTNER	FEMALE PARTNER	COUNTRY
1980	David Sycamore	Denise Weavers	Great Britain
1981	David Sycamore	Denise Weavers	Great Britain
1982: no competition held			
1983	David Sycamore	Denise Weavers	Great Britain
1984	David Sycamore	Denise Weavers	Great Britain
1985	David Sycamore	Denise Weavers	Great Britain
1986	Marcus Hilton	Karen Hilton	Great Britain
1987	Michael Hull	Patsy Hull-Krogull	Germany
1988	Raymond Myhrengen	Gunn Myhrengen	Norway
1989	Michael Hull	Patsy Hull-Krogull	Germany
1990	Michael Hull	Patsy Hull-Krogull	Germany
1991	Horst Beer	Andrea Beer	Germany
1992	Horst Beer	Andrea Beer	Germany
1993	Martin Lamb	Alison Lamb	Great Britain
1994	Bo Jensen	Helle Loft Jensen	Denmark
1995	Kim Rygel	Cecilie Rygel	Norway
1996	Kim Rygel	Cecilie Rygel	Norway
1997	Gary McDonald	Diana McDonald	USA
1998	Michael Hull	Mirjam Zweijsen	Germany
1999	Alain Doucet	Anik Jolicoeur	Canada
2000	Alain Doucet	Anik Jolicoeur	Canada
2001	Alain Doucet	Anik Jolicoeur	Canada
2002	Alain Doucet	Anik Jolicoeur	Canada
2003	Adam Reeve	Karen Reeve	Iceland
2004	Alain Doucet	Anik Jolicoeur	Canada
2005	Alessandro Garofolo	Annamaria Bassano	Italy
2006	Stefano Fanasca	Michaela Battisti	Italy
2007	Sergej Diemke	Katerina Timofeeva	Germany
2008	Gherman Mustuc	Iveta Lukosiute	USA
2009	Gherman Mustuc	Iveta Lukosiute	USA

THE CARL ALAN AWARDS

I think that it is only right and fitting that we should mention here those awards, which honour dance in general, for I feel it is important to recognise that Ballroom Dancing is just one section of the world of dance; and it is the prestigious Carl Alan Awards which were first introduced in 1953 by Eric Morley and were named after the joint Chairmen of Mecca Entertainment Company, (which owned a large proportion of Great Britain's dance halls at the time), Carl Heimann and Alan Fairley, that do just that.

The Carl Alan Awards – affectionately known as 'The Oscars of the Dance World' – are held annually in the United Kingdom to honour those who have made a significant contribution to dance and theatre in the three specific sections of Freestyle, Theatre and Ballroom, and Latin and Sequence, with five categories in each section, those being: Performer's Award, Teacher's Award, Competitive Coach/Choreography Award, Outstanding Services to Dance Award and Lifetime Achievement Award.

Listed below are past recipients of the awards: Sadly, information for these awaards was not readily available and so there are the occasional unavoidable ommissions for which I apologise.

YEAR	AWARDED TO	AWARDED FOR
1953	Wally Fryer and Violet Barnes	Professional Dancers
	Constance Grant	Formation Teachers
	Victor Silvester	Contribution to Dancing
	Joe and Kathy Stead	Professional Dancers (Sequence)
1954	Sonny Binnick and Sally Brock	Professional Dancers
	Maurice Fletcher and Fay Burrows	Professional Dancers (Sequence)
	Olive Ripman	Formation Teachers
1955	Sonny Binnick and Sally Brock	Professional Dancers
	Constance Grant	Formation Teachers
	Alf Halford and Marjorie Robinson	Professional Dancers (Sequence)
	Victor Silvester	Contribution to Dancing
1956	Alf Davies and Julie Reaby	Professional Dancers
	Maurice Fletcher and Fay Burrows	Professional Dancers (Sequence)
	Victor Silvester	Contribution to Dancing
	Frank and Peggy Spencer	Formation Teachers

YEAR	AWARDED TO	AWARDED FOR
1957	Sonny Binnick and Sally Brock	Professional Dancers
	Courtnenay Castle	Contribution to Dancing
	Jack Rigby and Florence Newbegin	Professional Dancers (Sequence)
	Frank and Peggy Spencer	Formation Teachers
1958	Kai Jensen	Overseas Award
	Harry Smith-Hampshire and Doreen Casey	Professional Dancers
	Philip JS Richardson OBE	Contribution to Dancing
	Jack Rigby and Florence Newbegin	Professional Dancers (Sequence)
	Frank and Peggy Spencer	Formation Teachers
1959	Desmond Ellison and Brenda Winslade	Professional Dancers
	Harold Hulley and Doreen Edwards	Professional Dancers (Sequence)
	Alex Moore	Contribution to Dancing
	Micky Powell	Overseas Award
	James Stevenson	
1960	Bob Burgess and Doreen Freeman	Professional Dancers
	Billy Butlin	Contribution to Dancing
	Constance Grant	Formation Teachers
	Frank Noble and Nora Bray	Professional Dancers (Sequence)
	Helen Wicks-Reid	Overseas Award
1961	Eric Beuss	Overseas Award
	Jack and Joyce Briggs	Professional Dancers (Sequence)
	Peter Eggleton and Brenda Winslade	Professional Dancers
	James and Gertrude Stevenson	Formation Teachers
	Peter West	Contribution to Dancing
1962	Wim Bonel	Overseas Award
	Arthur Franks	Contribution to Dancing
	Bill and Bobbie Irvine	Professional Dancers
	Ada Unsworth	Formation Teachers
	Ken Park and Mavis Whiteside	Professional Dancers (Sequence)
1963	Josephine Bradley	Special Award
	Evening News	Contribution to Dancing
	Kosaku Fujimura	Overseas Award
	Bill and Bobbie Irvine	Professional Dancers
	Ken Park and Mavis Whiteside	Professional Dancers (Sequence)
	Doreen Weeks	Formation Teachers

YEAR	AWARDED TO	AWARDED FOR
1964	Carl Carlsen	Overseas Award
	Laird and Lorraine	Professional Dancers
	Freddie Pederson	Formation Teachers
	Syd Perkin	Teachers
	Elsa Wells	Contribution to Dancing
	Lewis and Joan Wilson	Professional Dancers (Sequence)
1965	Peter Eggleton and Brenda Winslade	Professional Dancers
	Constance Grant	Teachers
	Richard and Lucy Keller	Overseas Award
	Leonard Morgan	Contribution to Dancing
	Frank and Peggy Spencer	Formation Teachers
	David and Gillian Stead	Professional Dancers (Sequence)
	John and Betty Westley	Amateur Dancers
1966	Fred Dieselhorst	Overseas Award
	Bill and Bobbie Irvine	Professional Dancers
	Philip Lewis	Contribution to Dancing
	Alex Moore	Teachers
	Frank and Peggy Spencer	Formation Teachers
	Derek Young and Shelia Buckley	Professional Dancers (Sequence)
1967	Thomas Bus	Overseas Award
	Mervyn Higgins and June Hunt	Amateur Dancers
	Peter Eggleton and Brenda Winslade	Professional Dancers
	Sybil Marks	Formation Teachers
	Peggy Spencer	Contribution to Dancing
	Bill Tasker	Teachers
	Lewis and Joan Wilson	Professional Dancers (Sequence)
1968	Ernie and Myra Chat	Amateur Dancers
	Nina Hunt	Teachers
	Bill and Bobbie Irvine MBE	Professional Dancers
	Frank and Peggy Spencer	Formation Teachers
	Rudolph Trautz	Overseas Award
	Glyn and Anne Watkins	Professional Dancers (Sequence)
1969	Richard and Janet Gleave	Amateur Dancers
	Anthony Hurley and Fay Saxton	Professional Dancers
	Stanley Jackson	Formation Teachers
	Albert van Lingen	Overseas Award

YEAR	AWARDED TO	AWARDED FOR
	Billy Martin	Teachers
	Jimmy Saville	Special Award
	Glyn and Anne Watkins	Professional Dancers (Sequence)
1970	Jack Briggs	Formation Teachers
	Gerd Hadrich	Overseas Award
	Leonard Morgan	Teachers
	Eric Morley	Contribution to Dancing
	Michael and Monica Needham	Professional Dancers
	Stan Shippy and Iris Kane	Amateur Dancers
	Alan Smith	Teachers
	Glyn and Anne Watkins	Professional Dancers (Sequence)
1971	Michael Barr and Vicky Green	Amateur Dancers
	Maurice Fletcher	Teachers
	Bob Garganico	Contribution to Dancing
	Anthony Hurley and Fay Saxton	Professional Dancers
	Joe Jenkins	Overseas Award
	Roy Mavor	Formation Teachers
	John and Betty Westley	Professional Dancers
	Olga Wilmot	Teachers
1972	Alan and Hazel Fletcher	Amateur Dancers
	Richard and Janet Gleave	Professional Dancers
	John Knight	Teachers
	Joe Loves	Overseas Award
	Wolfgang Optiz	Formation Teachers
	Wilfred Orange	Contribution to Dancing
	Cecil Ruault	Teachers
1973	Jeff and Muriel Aldren	Professional Dancers (Sequence)
	Renee Anderson	Formation Teachers
	Richard and Janet Gleave	Professional Dancers
	John Monte	Overseas Award
	Elizabeth Romain	Teachers
	Frank Venables and Linda Horwood	Amateur Dancers
	Alex Warren	Contribution to Dancing
1974	Jim Hall and Denise Mayo	Professional Dancers (Sequence)
	Phyllis Haylor	Special Award
	Detlef Hegemann	Overseas Award

YEAR	AWARDED TO	AWARDED FOR
	Peter Maxwell and Lynn Harman	Amateur Dancers
	Eric Morley	Contribution to Dancing
	Len Scrivener	Teachers
	Michael Stylianos and Lorna Lee	Professional Dancers
1975	Glenn and Lynette Boyce	Amateur Dancers
	Barrie Edgar	Contribution to Dancing
	Hans-Pieter Fischer	Overseas Award
	Richard and Janet Gleave	Professional Dancers
	John and Joan Knight	Formation Teachers
	Alex Moore	Special Award
	Roy and Linda Muldoon	Professional Dancers (Sequence)
	Robin and Rita Short	Professional Dancers
1976	Sonny Binick	Contribution to Dancing
	Keith and Judy Clifton	Amateur Dancers
	Gunter Dresen	Formation Teachers
	Peter Maxwell and Lynn Harman	Professional Dancers
	Leonard Morgan	Special Award
	Wayne and Wendy Packard	Professional Dancers (Sequence)
1977	Alan and Hazel Fletcher	Professional Dancers
	Kosaku Fujimura	Overseas Award
	Eric Higgins	Teachers (Sequence)
	Stanley Jackson	Formation Teachers
	Eric Morley	Special Award
	Gary Waite and Jennifer Pople	Professional Dancers (Sequence)
	Greg Smith and Marion Alleyne	Amateur Dancers
	Terry Wogan	Contribution to Dancing
1978	Michael and Vicky Barr	Professional Dancers
	Wim Bonel	Overseas Award
	Ted Burroughs	Formation Teachers
	Stephen Hillier and Lindsey Tate	Amateur Dancers
	Bobbie Irvine MBE	Special Award
	Stan Ross	Teachers (Sequence)
	Victor Silvester OBE	Contribution to Dancing (Posthumously)
	Peggy Spencer MBE	Teachers
	David Sycamore and Denise Weavers	Amateur Dancers

YEAR	AWARDED TO	AWARDED FOR
1979	HIH Prince Mikasa of Japan	Overseas Award
	Donnie Burns and Gaynor Fairweather	Amateur Dancers
	Barry and Susan Earnshaw	Professional Dancers (Sequence)
	Richard and Janet Gleave	Professional Dancers
	Flora Millar	Formation Teachers
	Alex Moore MBE	Special Award
	Harry Rollins	Teachers
1980	Josephine Bradley	Special Award
	Nancy Clarke	Teachers (Sequence)
	Harry Korner	Formation Teachers
	Walter Laird	Teachers
	Hans and Anne Laxholm	Amateur Dancers
	Wilfred Orange	Contribution to Dancing
	Espen and Kirsten Salberg	Professional Dancers
	Gary and Patricia Waite	Professional Dancers (Sequence)
	Robert Wrightson	Overseas Award
1981	Bob Dale	Formation Dancers
	Gilbert Daniels	Teachers
	Alan and Hazel Fletcher	Professional Dancers
	Kenny Welsh and Kathy Gilmartin	Amateur Dancers
	Eric Hancox	Teachers
	Doris Lavelle	Special Award
	Leonard Morgan	Contribution to Dancing
	Sidney Wells	Contribution to Dancing (Am)
	Professor Marian Wieczysty	Overseas Award
1982	David Bullen	Teachers (Sequence)
	Sidney Francis	Teachers
	Marcus Hilton and Karen Johnstone	Amateur Dancers
	Peter McLaughlan	Contribution to Dancing (Am)
	Eric Morley	Special Award
	Meryem Pearson	Overseas Award
	Bobby Short	Special Award
	Sammy and Shirley Stopford	Professional Dancers
	Michael Stylianos	Contribution to Dancing
	Jurgen and Petra Zumholte	Formation Teachers

YEAR	AWARDED TO	AWARDED FOR
1983	Leonard Morgan	Contribution to Dancing
	Wayne and Wendy Packard	Professional Dancers (Sequence)
	Bobby Philp	Special Award
	Ella Scutts	Special Award
	Tony Smith	Formation Teachers
	David Sycamore and Denise Weavers	Professional Dancers
	Rita Thomas	Contribution to Dancing (Am)
	Benny Tolmeyer	Teachers
	Rudi Trautz	Overseas Award
	John Wood and Heather Stuart	Amateur Dancers
1984–1992: no awards presented between these years		
1993	Fred Bijster	Overseas Award
	Freddie Boultwood	Professional Who Did Most for Dance (Standard Latin and Sequence)
	Jack Briggs	Teachers (Sequence)
	Warren Bullock and Jane Philips	Amateur (Standard)
	Joanna Bungay	Amateur (Ballet)
	Bob Burgess	Teachers (Standard)
	Donnie Burns MBE and Gaynor Fairweather MBE	Outstanding Services to Dance
	Donnie Burns MBE and Gaynor Fairweather MBE	Professional Competitors (Latin)
	John Byrnes and Jane Lyttleton	Amateur (Latin)
	Roy Castle	Professional Who Did Most for Dance (Stage – Ballet and Tap)
	Donna Classey	Amateur (Modern – Stage)
	Janet Clark	Professional Who Did Most for Dance (Disco and Freestyle)
	Dorothy Coates	Special Award
	Frances Dawson	Teachers (Disco and Freestyle))
	Mary Edwards	Special Award
	Michael O'Callaghan and Emma Dodds	Amateur (Sequence Old Time)
	Mark Paton and Jacqui Davis	Professional Competitors (Sequence)

YEAR	AWARDED TO	AWARDED FOR
	Marcus and Karen Hilton	Professional Competitors (Standard)
	Helen Rose	Amateur (Modern)
	Bobby Short	Special Award
	Sadie Simpson	Teachers (Stage)
	Michael Stylianos	Teachers (Latin)
1994	Roger Billington	Special Award
	Paul Brookes	Amateur Award (Disco Freestyle)
	Jean Cantell	Teachers (Disco and Freestyle)
	Emily Chadburn	Special Award
	Richard and Lisa Dyke	Amateur Award (Rock 'n' Roll)
	Julie Earnshaw	Teachers (Sequence)
	Ella Hardy	Teachers (Stage)
	Robert Harold	Professional Who Did Most for Dance
	Russell Heppenstall and Michelle Prigmore	Professional Competitors (Sequence)
	Adrian Hibberd and Jenny Grew	Amateur Award (Sequence Old Time)
	Nigel Horrocks	Professional Who Did Most for Dance
	Corrie van Hugten	Overseas Award
	Anthony Hurley	Teachers (Standard)
	Rebecca Jackson	Amateur Award (Ballet)
	Keith Jones	Special Award
	Joanna Kilminster	Amateur Award (Tap)
	Mark Lucas and Delia Crossley	Amateur Award (Standard)
	Mark Lunn and Jannie Baltzer	Amateur Award (Latin)
	Natalie Morris	Amateur Award (Modern – Stage)
	Margaret Redmond	Teachers (Latin)
	Augustus Schiavo and Caterina Arzenton	Professional Competitors (Standard)
	Robin Short	Professional Who Did Most for Dance
	Sammy Stopford and Barbara McColl	Professional Competitors (Latin)

YEAR	AWARDED TO	AWARDED FOR
	Rita Thomas	Special Award
	Leanne Thompson	
1995	Corky and Shirley Ballas	Professional Competitors (Latin)
	Bonnie Barr	Professional Who Did Most for Dance (Disco and Freestyle)
	Ted and Sue Burroughs	Teachers (Sequence)
	Bob Dale	Teachers (Standard)
	Joanne Denham	Amateur (Ballet)
	John Francis and Susan Pyatt	Amateur (Rock 'n' Roll)
	Robert Finnigan and Johanne Lloyd	Amateur (Sequence Old Time)
	Len Goodman	Teachers (Disco and Freestyle)
	Geoffrey Hearn	Teachers (Latin)
	Detlef Hegemann	Overseas Award
	Marcus and Karen Hilton	Professional Competitors (Standard)
	Timothy Howson and Joanne Bolton	Amateur (Standard)
	Rebecca Jackson	Amateur (Modern – Stage)
	Ross Mitchell	Special Award
	Edna Murphy	Professional Who Did Most for Dance (Standard Latin and Sequence)
	Darren Park and Andrea Kilgour	Professional Competitors (Sequence)
	Tina Parkes	Amateur (Disco and Freestyle)
	Paul Richardson and Lorna Dawson	Amateur (Latin)
	Angela Rippon	Special Award
	Jessie Stewart	Professional Teachers
	Dougie Squires	Professional Who Did Most for Dance (Ballet and Tap)
	Bill Tasker	Special Award
	Leanne Thompson	Amateur (Tap)
1996	Luca Baricchi and Lorraine Barry	Professional Competitors (Standard)
	Nora Billington	Special Award
	Philip and Helen Blackburn	Professional Competitors (Sequence)

YEAR	AWARDED TO	AWARDED FOR
	Margaret Cox	Teachers (Stage)
	Matthew and Nicole Cutler	Amateur (Latin)
	Geoff David	Professional Who Did Most for Dance (Stage – Ballet and Tap)
	Lilian Dooley	Overseas Award
	Sydney Francis	Special Award
	Paul Hill and Jennifer Grew	Amateur (Sequence Old Time)
	Lizzie Grunsell	Amateur (Modern – Stage)
	Christopher Hawkins and Hazel Newberry	Amateur (Standard)
	Jean Johnson	Teachers (Sequence)
	Anna Jones	Teachers (Disco and freestyle)
	John Leach	Special Award
	Christopher Lewis	Amateur (Ballet)
	Nicola and Rosalind Lynch	Amateur (Disco and Freestyle) Amateur (Rock 'n' Roll)
	Natalie Morris	Amateur (Tap)
	Yvonne Taylor-Hill	Professional Who Did Most for Dance (Disco and Freestyle)
	Pat Thompson	Teachers (Latin)
	Frank Venables	Teachers (Standard)
	Lyndon Wainwright	Professional Who Did Most for Dance (Standard, Latin and Sequence)
	Bryan Watson and Karen Hardy	Professional Competitors (Latin)
1997	Bryan Allen	Professional Who Did Most for Dance
	Lilian Aubrey	Teachers (Disco and Freestyle)
	Craig Bedwell and Angela Painting	Amateur (Sequence Old Time)
	Paul Beeton	Teachers (Latin)
	Fred Bijster	Overseas Award
	Philip and Helen Blackburn	Teachers (Sequence)
	Nancy Clarke	Teachers (Sequence)
	Frances Dawson	Professional Who Did Most for Dance
	Robert Falshaw	Special Award

YEAR	AWARDED TO	AWARDED FOR
	Jukka Haapalainen and Sirpa Suutari	Teachers (Latin)
	Graeme Henderson	Professional Award
	Marcus and Karen Hilton MBE	Professional Competitors (Standard)
	Gill MacKenzie	Special Award
	Kristen McNally	Amateur (Ballet)
	Stan Page	Teachers (Standard)
	Michael Parkinson	Amateur (Modern – Stage)
	Nicholas Rogers and Andrea Crockfield	Amateur (Rock 'n' Roll)
	Alan and Donna Shingler	Amateur (Standard)
	Barbara Tucker	Special Award
	David Watson and Malin Karlsson	Amateur (Latin)
	Joanna Yuille	Amateur (Tap)
	Gerry Zuccarello	Teachers (Stage)
1998	Adam Billingham and Zoe Smith	Professional Competitors (Sequence)
	Freddie Boultwood	Special Award
	George Coad	Teachers (Standard)
	Len Colyer	Special Award
	Hayley Conway	Teachers (Disco and Freestyle)
	Jonathan Crossley and Kylie Jones	Amateur (Standard)
	Matthew and Nicole Cutler	Amateur (Latin)
	Jennifer Ellison	Amateur (Ballet)
	Derek Green	Who Did Most for Dance (Disco and Freestyle)
	Kate Goldey	Amateur (Disco and Freestyle)
	Jukka Haapalainen and Sirpa Suutari	Professional Competitors (Latin)
	Marcus and Karen Hilton MBE	Professional Competitors (Standard)
	Rudi Hubert	Overseas
	Michael and Margaret Jeffries	Amateur (Sequence Old Time)
	Walter Laird	Teachers (Latin)
	Ian McLeod	Teachers (Stage)
	Kerry Platts	Amateur (Modern)

YEAR	AWARDED TO	AWARDED FOR
	Amy Ellen Richardson	Amateur(Tap)
	Jean Rowbotham	Special Award
	Jackie Sanderson	Teachers (Sequence)
	Robin Short	Who Did Most for Dance (Standard, Latin and Sequence)
	Craig Walker and Kirstie Allen	Amateur (Rock 'n' Roll)
	Phil Winston	Who Did Most for Dance (Stage – Ballet and Tap)
1999	Len Armstrong	Teachers (Standard)
	Freddie Boultwood	Special Award
	Stephen Buck	Teachers (Disco)
	Jacqui Donaldson	Special Award
	Rosemary Ford	Professional Award
	Veronica Hamill	Outstanding Services to Dance
	Peggy Harrison	Teachers (Professional)
	Gill MacKenzie	Special Award
	Bill Phillips	Special Award
	Wayne Sleep	Outstanding Services to Dance
	Rita Thomas	Special Award
	Pat Thompson	Teachers (Latin)
	Derek Tonks	Teachers (Sequence)
	Lyndon Wainwright	Special Award

Presented by Stage Dance Council International

2000	Jean Geddes	Teachers (Professional)
	Audrey Griffiths	Professional Award
	Hilda Hylton-Bromley	Outstanding Services to Dance
	Harriet Skipper	Outstanding Services to Dance
2001	Norah Button	Outstanding Services to Dance
	John Harrison	Outstanding Services to Dance
	Lorette Legge	Professional Award
	Barbara Woff	Teachers (Professional)
2002	Lilian Aubrey	Outstanding Services to Dance
	Graeme Henderson	Professional Award
	Barbara Sharples	Outstanding Services to Dance
	Judith Silvester	Teachers (Professional)

YEAR	AWARDED TO	AWARDED FOR
2003	Colin Lang	Professional Award
	Glenys McGill	Teachers (Professional) and Outstanding Services to Dance
	Margaret Walls	Outstanding Services to Dance

Presented and Sponsored by Nigel and Janice Horrocks Promotions

2000	Stephen and Denise Green	
	Kenneth Lee	
	Donna Wyatt	

Presented by Nigel and Janice Horrocks Promotions Sponsored by the United Kingdom Alliance

2001	Gillian Anderson	Teacher (Disco/Freestyle Dance)
	Dawn Barrett	Team Trainer (Disco/Freestyle Dance)
	John and Charlotte Comrie	Promoters (Disco/Freestyle Dance)
	Derek Green	Outstanding Contribution (Disco/Freestyle Dance)
	June Green	Teachers (Disco/Freestyle Dance)
	David Jones	Special Award (Disco/Freestyle Dance)
	Derek Mayes	Teachers (Disco/Freestyle Dance)
	Iris Mayes	Special Award (Disco/Freestyle Dance)
2002	David Boyd	Outstanding Contribution (Disco/Freestyle Dance)
	Jean Cantell	Special Award (Disco/Freestyle Dance)
	Chris Green	Teachers (Disco/Freestyle Dance)
	Sinead Hickman	Teachers (Disco/Freestyle Dance)
	David and Anna Jones	Promoters (Disco/Freestyle Dance)
	Stephen and Stephanie Jones	Team Trainers (Disco/Freestyle Dance)
	Karen Llewellyn	Special Award (Disco/Freestyle Dance)
	Paul Streatfield	Teachers (Disco/Freestyle Dance)
2003	Anita Brown	Team Trainers (Disco/Freestyle Dance)
	Tony Curley	Teachers (Disco/Freestyle Dance)
	Frances Dawson	Special Award (Disco/Freestyle Dance)
	Nigel Horrocks	Special Award (Disco/Freestyle Dance)
	Nigel and Janice Horrocks	Promoters (Disco/Freestyle Dance)

YEAR	AWARDED TO	AWARDED FOR
	Barbara Johnson	Teachers (Disco/Freestyle Dance)
	Glenys Mc Gill	Outstanding Services to Dance
	Rosemary Oaks	Outstanding Contribution (Disco/Freestyle Dance)
	Karen Stewart	Teachers (Disco/Freestyle Dance)
	Margaret Walls	Outstanding Services to Dance

Presented by Dance News Special Projects Ltd. Sponsored by the International Dance Teachers' Association

2001 *(Presented January 2002)*

	Rudi Baumann	Outstanding Lifetime Achievement
	Karl Breuer	Outstanding Lifetime Achievement
	Peter Dobner	Outstanding Lifetime Achievement
	Mick Free	Outstanding Lifetime Achievement
	John Kimmins	Outstanding Lifetime Achievement
	John Knight	Outstanding Lifetime Achievement
	Rita Thomas	Outstanding Lifetime Achievement
	Norman White	Outstanding Lifetime Achievement

2002 *(Presented January 2003)*

	Ken Bateman and Blanche Ingle	Outstanding Lifetime Achievement
	Doreen Freeman	Outstanding Lifetime Achievement
	Bill and Bobbie Irvine MBE	Outstanding Lifetime Achievement
	Borge Jensen	Outstanding Lifetime Achievement
	Isao Nakagawa	Outstanding Lifetime Achievement

2003 *(Presented January 2004)*

Peter Eggleton
Adalberto and Lalla Dell 'Orto
Rene Barsi
Alan and Hazel Fletcher
Kathy Oldland
Jack Reavely

2004 *(Presented January 2005)*

Freddie Boultwood
Lesley Garrett CBE
Edith Kershaw

YEAR	AWARDED TO	AWARDED FOR
	Gill MacKenzie	
	Michael Stylianos and Lorna Lee	
2005–2006: no awards were presented during this period		
2007	Timothy Howson and Joanne Bolton	Ballroom, Latin and Sequence Performer's Award
	Anna Jane Casey	Stage/Theatre Performer's
	Tony Bill	Freestyle Lifetime Achievement
	Sue Burroughs	Ballroom, Latin and Sequence Competitive Coach
	Hilda Hylton-Bromley	Stage/Theatre Lifetime Achievement
	Jill Kemp	Freestyle Teacher's
	John and Arlene Leach	Ballroom, Latin and Sequence Lifetime Achievement
	Patricia Lupino Thompson	Stage/Theatre Teacher's
	Stephen Mear	Stage/Theatre Coach/Choreographer
	Philip Perry	Ballroom, Latin and Sequence Teacher's
	Arlene Phillips	Stage/Theatre Outstanding Services to Dance
	Lori Silmon	Freestyle Performer's
	Garry Waite	Freestyle Outstanding Services to Dance
	Philip Wylie	Ballroom, Latin and Sequence Outstanding Services to Dance
	Samantha Williams	Freestyle Competitive Coach
2008	Darren Bennett and Lilia Kopylova	Ballroom, Latin and Sequence Performer's
	Jack Briggs	Ballroom, Latin and Sequence Lifetime Achievement
	Darcey Bussell CBE	Stage/Theatre Performers
	George Coad	Ballroom, Latin and Sequence Competitive Coach
	Freda Compton MBE	Stage/Theatre Lifetime Achievement
	Vicky Cooper	Freestyle Competitive Coach
	Jilly Harris	Freestyle Teacher's

YEAR	AWARDED TO	AWARDED FOR
	Paul Harris	Stage/Theatre Coach/Choreographer
	Beryl Hill	Freestyle Lifetime Achievement
	Keith Holmes	Ballroom, Latin and Sequence Outstanding Services to Dance
	Alan and Joan Merrall	Ballroom, Latin and Sequence Teacher's
	Nicky Miles	Freestyle Outstanding Services to Dance
	Aaron Morgan	Freestyle Performers
	Judith Thompson	Stage/Theatre Teacher's
	Shirley Thompson Bradley	Stage/Theatre Outstanding Services to Dance
2009	Lauren Mac Auley	Freestyle Performer
	Russell Sargeant	Theatre Performer
	Michael Malitowski and Joanna Leunis	Ballroom, Latin and Sequence Performers
	Maggie Quilietti	Freestyle Teacher
	Annette Bromley	Theatre Teacher
	Warren and Jane Bullock	Ballroom, Latin and Sequence Teacher's
	Gillian Anderson	Freestyle Competitive Coach
	Phil Winston	Theatre Choreographer
	Margaret Redmond	Ballroom, Latin and Sequence Competitive Coach
	Yvonne Taylor-Hill	Freestyle Outstanding Services to Dance
	Derek Young	Theatre Outstanding Services to Dance
	Joy Weller	Ballroom, Latin and Sequence Outstanding Services to Dance
	David Roberts	Freestyle Lifetime Achievement
	Bruce Forsyth	Theatre Lifetime Achievement
	Joan Field	Ballroom, Latin and Sequence Lifetime Achievement
2010	Joanne McPhee	Freestyle performer
	Adam Booth	Theatre Performer

YEAR	AWARDED TO	AWARDED FOR
	Jonathan and Hazel Newberry MBE	Ballroom and Latin Sequence Performer's
	Lyn Bill	Freestyle Teacher's
	Emma Whyte	Theatre Teacher's
	Mark and Jayne Shutlar	Ballroom, Latin and Sequence Teacher's
	Bonnie Barr	Freestyle Competitive Coach
	Jayne Torvill and Christopher Dean	Theatre Coach/Choreographer
	Stephen Hillier MBE	Ballroom, Latin and Sequence Competitive Coach
	Jackie Sanderson	Outstanding Services to Dance (Freestyle)
	Jessie Stewart-Haggarty MBE	Outstanding Services to Dance (Theatre)
	Ann Green	Outstanding Services to Dance (Ballroom Latin and Sequence)
	Stephen and Stephanie Jones	Lifetime Achievement (Freestyle)
	Dame Beryl Grey	Lifetime Achievement (Theatre)
	Rita Pover	Lifetime Achievement (Ballroom Latin and Sequence)

When one is fortunate, or should I say 'talented', enough to receive an award, it is to some extent important who actually presents that award, for the status of the presenter is in some way a reflection of the status of the award itself, for it stands to reason that a low level award would not attract a high level presenter, does it not? On that note then the list of presenters for the Carl Alan Awards is an impressive read indeed and in the past has included the likes of: Alicia Markova, Dame Margot Fonteyn, Dame Sybil Thorndike, Duke and Duchess of Kent, Duke of Edinburgh, Prince Charles, Prince Michael of Kent, Prince Rainier and Princess Grace, Princess Anne and Princess Margaret.

AN ENTERTAINMENT LEGEND CALLED BRUCE FORSYTH

Some may question why I have decided to include Bruce Forsyth in a book on Ballroom Dancing; they may say to me he is not a champion dancer, well a champion he may not be, but a dancer he most certainly is. In fact Bruce Forsyth is everything to everyone in the world of entertainment; he can do it all, including Ballroom Dancing, and the man sure can dance – even now, in his eighties!

Bruce *is* Mr Entertainment and Ballroom is entertaining, but most importantly he has played a huge part in the success of the television show *Strictly Come Dancing* which has brought the joys of Ballroom Dancing to the masses, not just nationally but internationally too. A book on Ballroom Dancing, therefore, that did not include Bruce Forsyth would be incomplete, and so here he is, where he belongs, where it's *'nice to see him, to see him – NICE!'*.

BRUCE FORSYTH

National Treasure, Entertainment Legend and the King of Catchphrases who is lovingly known to the nation as 'Brucie'

BRUCE FORSYTH: The Man and His Life

- Bruce Joseph Forsyth-Johnson, (to give 'Brucie' his full name), was born on 22 February 1928 in Edmonton, London to John, a local garage owner, and Florence, who was the lead vocalist with the Salvation Army
- He was educated at the Latymer School in Edmonton
- In 1942 he began his entertainment career as Boy Bruce – the Mighty Atom, a song, dance and accordion act
- In 1949, at the age of 21, he appeared at London's Windmill Theatre, the home of non-stop nude revue
- When he was 25 years old he married Penny Calvert, one of the dancers he met when they were both appearing at the Windmill Theatre. She was 23
- They went on to have three daughters together, Debbie, Julie and Laura
- 1958 was the turning point in Bruce Forsyth's career for in that year he was booked as a compère on the TV show *Sunday Night at the London Palladium*

- He was initially booked for just two weeks, but stayed on for five years, and as a result became the resident star of the show and will be forever remembered for his part in the popular game show *Beat the Clock* – well by those old enough to remember it, that is! This game show gave rise to his catchphrase '*Good game, good game*'
- In 1964 Bruce met Ann Sidney and his marriage to Penny came to an end
- In the same year he starred in the West End musical *Little Me* at the Cambridge Theatre
- In 1973, five months after his eventual divorce from Penny, Bruce married Anthea Redfern, 25 years his junior and the hostess on the hugely popular Saturday night TV show *The Generation Game*; it was her appearance in beautiful clothes, and often short skirts displaying her lovely long legs, that gave rise to another of his now famous catchphrases: '*Give us a twirl, Anthea*'
- Bruce and Anthea went on to have two daughters together, Charlotte and Louisa, before divorcing in 1979
- In 1980 he was invited to judge the Miss World competition, and once more the love bug bit him when he met Wilnelia Merced, another of the judges. The beautiful Puerto Rican was a former Miss World herself, having won the contest in 1975, and was 31 years Bruce's junior
- In 1983 Bruce and Wilnelia were married in New York
- In 1986 their son, Jonathon Joseph, 'JJ', was born
- In 1998 Bruce Forsyth was awarded the OBE for his outstanding work in the world of entertainment
- 2004 was another defining moment in his career when he was invited to host what was to become another British institution the television show *Strictly Come Dancing*, a show that was also set to become an international success – it also established another three catchphrases: '*You're my favourite,*' '*I am not doddery, doddery I am – not!*' and '*I'll clear this place*'
- 2005 was a busy year for Bruce Forsyth, for not only had it become evident that *Strictly Come Dancing* was destined to go global, but it was the year in which he performed live, in the presence of HM the Queen and the Royal Family, for BBC1 at the Festival of Commemoration, which celebrated the 60th anniversary of the end of the World War II. It was also the year in which a bronze bust of Bruce Forsyth was unveiled in the Cinderella Bar at the London Palladium, celebrating his six

decades in the entertainment industry but, most importantly, it was also the year in which he was awarded the CBE
• 2007 saw Bruce travelling to Las Vegas for BBC1's one-hour production special *Bruce Does Vegas* which told the story of his fellow performing legends, British and American, past and present; such legendary entertainers as Elvis Presley, Liberace and the Rat Pack, who have helped make Las Vegas the entertainment capital of the world were included
• In 2008 Bruce Forsyth received BAFTA's highest accolade, the Academy Fellowship

BRUCE'S POPULAR TV SHOWS INCLUDE:

Bruce Forsyth's Big Night
The Generation Game
Play Your Cards Right
The Price is Right
Strictly Come Dancing
Sunday Night at the London Palladium
You Bet!

BRUCE'S CATCHPHRASES INCLUDE:

'*Didn't he do well!*'
'*Give us a twirl, Anthea.*'
'*Good game, good game.*'
'*I am not doddery, doddery I am – not!*'
'*I'll clear this place.*'
'*I'm in charge.*'
'*Nice to see you, to see you nice.*'
'*What a lovely audience! You're so much better than last week.*'
'*You don't get anything for a pair – not in this game.*'
'*You're my favourite.*'

BRUCE'S AWARDS INCLUDE:

BCA's Top BBC Entertainment Presenter
Carl Alan Award (Theatre Performers Award)

Favourite Game Show Host (as voted by the readers of the TV Times magazine on three separate occasions)
Favourite TV Personality (as voted by the readers of the TV Times magazine on three occasions)
Royal Television Society's Lifetime Achievement Award
Showbusiness Personality of the Year (Awarded by The Variety Club of Great Britain)
Star in the walkway of stars in London
TV Personality of the Year

AND FINALLY ...

- To date Bruce has compèred and appeared in no fewer than 12 Royal Variety shows
- Bruce Forsyth is the gentleman entertainer who, in a liberal age, is never rude, offensive or unpleasant and who never uses bad language; Bruce Forsyth shows us all that decency can succeed and more importantly it can enjoy enduring success, so let that be a lesson to us all

* * *

BLACKPOOL AND BALLROOM

The word 'Blackpool' is synonymous with Ballroom Dancing.

Blackpool is an English seaside town that anyone and everyone who is interested in Ballroom Dancing must visit at least just once, in order to enjoy the complete experience.

The Town of Blackpool

The town of Blackpool on the North-West coast of England is essentially a typical English seaside town and is famous not only for its Tower Ballroom and Winter Gardens – both being homes to Ballroom Dancing competitions – but also for its Golden Mile of amusements, for the romantic trams that run along the promenade, (Blackpool has the distinction of having the oldest street tramway in the world), and of course for its landladies. Blackpool landladies are, you see, a special breed of landladies. Infamous throughout the land, they are reputed to be, and renowned as, a formidable bunch of ladies who run the local guest houses with a military precision! Stories abound about the landladies and there are even postcards depicting them and their guesthouses.

Blackpool Tower
Opened on 14 May 1894 Blackpool Tower is the English version of the Eiffel Tower in Paris and has become arguably 'the' most famous of British seaside landmarks.

The Ballroom
In 1899 the Tower Ballroom was opened and destined to become famous in the world of Ballroom Dancing. Now every afternoon, throughout the summer season tea dances are held in this Ballroom.

The Winter Gardens
The Winter Gardens, Blackpool is home to the country's second largest theatre – the Opera House with a seating capacity of almost 3000. Four of the five Dance Festivals are held in the Empress Ballroom at the Winter Gardens, whilst the Junior Dance Festival is held at the Blackpool Tower Ballroom.

The Dance Festivals
One could say that Blackpool is the epicentre of Ballroom Dancing and even if you are not, as they say, 'good enough' to be a contestant at Blackpool, if you are interested in Ballroom Dancing then it is like a magnet and will pull you in.

The first Blackpool Dance Festival was held in 1920 in the Winter Gardens' Empress Ballroom but in content was far removed from the contests of today and later went through many transitional phases to become the international success and home of Ballroom as we now know it.

As far back as the 1930s there were very strong Ballroom Dance ties with Denmark but it wasn't until the 1950s that the real influx of foreign competitors began. At this stage a special box on the south balcony in the Ballroom was reserved for foreign visitors, and this is the way it remained until 1980 when the box was discontinued as by this stage the sheer number of foreign competitors made it impractical and impossible to accommodate

Blackpool is known the world over as the home of Ballroom Dancing and the Tower Ballroom as the place to 'twirl'. (visitBlackpool)

the volume of resulting visitors. The increase in numbers has continued over the years with as many as fifty competing countries.

So internationally popular was the dance festival in Blackpool that it was eventually decided to organise a smaller festival for British competitors only and so in 1975 the first British Closed Dance festival was held in the Empress Ballroom. The name, however, has since been changed to the British National Championships.

The Five Blackpool Dance Festivals

Each year the dancers of the world descend on Blackpool to share their talents and hopefully prove that they are the best in the world. There are five festivals in total:

The Junior Dance Festival

This festival began in 1947 and, until 2010, was held in the famous Blackpool Tower Ballroom after which it was moved to join its more grown up friends in the Winter Gardens.

The Blackpool Dance Festival

This festival is the largest of all the five Blackpool Festivals and began in 1920 in the Winter Gardens' Empress Ballroom. It runs for a total of nine days and covers both Ballroom and Latin American Dancing, incorporating:

* British Open Championships – Adult Amateur and Professional Couples Formation Teams
* British Rising Star Amateur Ballroom and Latin Competitions
* Professional Team Match
* Exhibition Competition

Less than 90 years after the start of this festival over 60 countries entered almost 2,000 competitors in the various events.

The Blackpool Freestyle Championships

This championship covers:

- solos
- teams
- slowdance
- street/hip-hop pairs, solos and couples

Blackpool Sequence Dance Festival
This festival covers:

- Classical Sequence
- Modern Sequence
- Latin Sequence

British National Dance Championships
The final festival is for British dance couples only in:

- Ballroom Dancing
- Latin American Dancing

It is said that you are only a fully fledged dancer when you have enjoyed the Blackpool experience!

BALLROOM ON THE TV

The Television Show *Strictly Come Dancing* is not a TV show, it is a TV phenomenon, and officially one of the most successful reality shows ever.

This is not the first time a television show based on Ballroom Dancing has enjoyed unprecedented success, for the forerunner, (some even say mother), of *Strictly Come Dancing* was that other television show based on Ballroom Dancing and called *Come Dancing*.

Come Dancing started its TV life in 1949 and was on and off the screen until 1995 thus becoming one of the television's longest running shows of all time. The brainchild of impresario Eric Morley, the TV show *Come Dancing* didn't begin life as a competition with that format until 1953. It was initially conceived as a way to bring the joys of dancing to the man in the street and so the early shows concentrated on teaching the required moves to each dance. Somehow I think such a mundane approach today would have viewers turning off their TV sets in their millions, instead of turning on which is in fact what they are doing for the new millenium version which is now called *Strictly Come Dancing*.

In 1953 the competition element was added; regional heats were held and broadcast from various Ballrooms around the country where winning through to the National Final was the aim. The result was that the show was a huge success. This early television show, however, lacked the glitz and the glamour of today, but then we do have to remember that when the programme began it was not only soon after the end of the Second World War, but it was also the early days of television too. In fact, relatively few homes had a television set when the programme was first broadcast with the boom in sales not taking place until many people bought a set to watch the coronation of Queen Elizabeth II. Add to this too the fact that programmes were broadcast in black and white. In those days, if you were one of the fortunate few to see the 'real' thing, you would have been astounded at the bizarre colours and perhaps wondered whether in fact the wardrobe department had suffered a fashion meltdown. Colours transmitted in black and white did not behave themselves and so contestants were told to dress in colours that would make clear definitions on screen – but in life would make you quite nauseous! This applied to all TV shows pre colour, I hasten to add, and not just to *Come Dancing*. For example, the white starched nurses' uniforms in the obligatory medical soap of the time, *Emergency Ward Ten*, were in fact yellow.

Another difference between the two shows is that a big part of the *Come Dancing* show was the Formation Section, whereas the *Strictly Come Dancing* competitive format has no place in which Formation Dancing can comfortably sit – yet! Then, for those who are old enough to remember it, there was the 'Off Beat' section, which was a modern dance format as far away from the rigidity, rules and regulations of the more formal Ballroom section as it was possible to be. It added another artistic dimension though and attracted the younger audience members too.

Strictly Come Dancing is the prime reason that Saturday night is no longer the 'Night to go out', as it has been for many decades, but has become instead the 'Night to stay in', at least in the autumn months, which is the transmission period for this particular show. And in the event that you do find a household where not everyone is a fan, it makes little difference, because someone will be and so that night out simply cannot happen. The non fan just has to kick his heels – almost a dance in itself! – and wait until the programme has finished.

And so, we have a programme that rules the nation's leisure time during the autumn/winter months of each year as a simple competitive, light entertainment programme based on the Dancesport of Ballroom Dancing, in which celebrity figures team up with experts in the field and try to out-dance each other by surviving a voting elimination process – in the hands of the viewing audience.

Beginning in 2004, and showing no signs of ending, the viewing figures for 'Strictly' have climbed each year to make it one of the most popular light entertainment programmes currently on television. It began its life in the UK but quickly became a global success – interestingly with a different name in many countries. For example, in Australia – the first to follow us – it is called *Dancing with the Stars*, whereas the Germans call it *Let's Dance*. In 2005 the US followed with their version also being called *Dancing with the Stars* and not only did they adopt the show format but also two of our judges, in the form of our cheeky, silver-tongued Eastender Len Goodman and Bruno Tonioli; Craig Revel Horwood, meanwhile, appeared on the New Zealand version so once again *Britannia rules the dance floor!*

ARTISTIC INCLINATIONS

My husband has a theory, and I think he is quite right, though I do question my wisdom at committing this admission to print! His theory is, however, that artistic individuals are rarely artistic in only one area and whilst the hand many be at the feast, the fingers are in many pies. He himself is a very talented musician, but he is also a magnificent chef; we similarly have a friend who in her prime danced with Nureyev and who also is a culinary expert, whilst another plays eight instruments and paints miniatures in his 'spare' time. Up until now this 'theory' has just served to amuse and fascinate us, but suddenly it took on more importance when writing this book, for it was then that I saw some paintings by a talented, well respected and award winning dance teacher, and the seed was sown. What could be more perfect than an actual dancer illustrating a book on dance? Nothing I can assure you. So who is she?

STEPHANIE JONES

The artist and the dancer

- Stephanie (Turner) was born in Rochdale, Lancashire as the only child of Chris and Joan Turner who ran Turners Dance Centre in Rochdale, and so I suppose one could say that genetically it was a pretty sure bet that Stephanie Turner would not have two left feet
- She was educated at Bury Grammar School, after which she went on to study Economics at Aston, University in Birmingham
- After graduating from Aston, her first teaching post was at Rochdale College, where she taught Economics
- This brought in the money to survive, but her heart was in dancing – proving that you can never kill a good gene!
- Now fully involved in her parents' dance school, she knew that she wanted to make this school different and one that would stand out from the thousands of other excellent dance schools around the country; and so it was that an idea began to grow
- Up until this point the school had concentrated on the mainstream dance classes of Modern Ballroom, Latin American and Rock 'n' Roll but Stephanie decided that the way forward was to entice fun loving youngsters into the school and stimulate their interest in dance through their seemingly "compulsory" love of, and fascination for, pop music
- Routines were created for these otherwise non dancers, and the result was that what started off as a one-class venture developed into a full time project
- Meanwhile, her own dancing 'career' was equally successful, as together with her first professional partner, Gary Sharpe (who was a junior Latin champion), she won the UK Disco Dance Championship on two consecutive years
- Stephanie and Gary then went on to compete, lecture and demonstrate Disco Latin Dancing
- Then in 1979 one of the IDTA examiners, Raymond Draper from Sheffield, introduced Stephanie to Steve Jones, who was at the time the British Youth Champion in Ballroom. Raymond thought that they would make good dancing partners, but what he didn't bargain for was Cupid's

Stephanie Jones – The Artist and the Dancer. (Reproduced with kind permission of Stephanie Jones)

intervention too, for when they met it was love at first sight for the pair of them

- At the time of their meeting Steve was a trainee solicitor, but he soon left his job to work at Turners Dance Centre with Stephanie
- In 1979 Stephanie Turner and Steve Jones were married, just nine months after they first met
- Life was good for the Jones' as Turners Dance Centre went from strength to strength and the routines created by Stephanie drew in teachers nationwide, wanting to be taught new routines by this talented lady and her new husband and dance partner
- The Jones's travelled both Nationally and Internationally teaching, lecturing and dancing in the Latin Disco Dance style. They also danced in the *'Off Beat' section* of *Come Dancing*, the fore-runner to the new equally popular TV series *Strictly Come Dancing*
- In 1985 their son Paul Michael, affectionately known as PM, was born – destined to be a dancer, of course
- Stephanie, meanwhile, kept working on her own personal project – a team of young disco performers called *Cheeky Bits* who amongst other appearances, appeared on the Royal Variety Show, ironically alongside another entertainer with a penchant for painting – Rolf Harris
- In 1997 and 1999 Stephanie and Steve Jones won Classique de Danse awards for Training Freestyle Dance Teams, following that with a Carl Alan award in 2002, again for Freestyle Training
- Then an earlier serious head on car collision in the year 1970 caught up with Stephanie and the original back injury she sustained at the time became more difficult to control, meaning that her successful and flourishing dance career was forced to slow down, a small price to pay though when one considers that she was thrown through the roof of her parents' car in a collision, which left her mother for dead; amazingly her mother, in fact, is still teaching today and Stephanie now has two artistic careers instead of just the one!
- She may have a degree in Economics, but it is the blood of art that runs through her veins, and so less dancing meant that she had to channel her artistic blood in other directions, and so she took up painting – for which I for one am eternally grateful!
- Together with Steve and her mother Joan, Stephanie continues to run Turner's Dance Centre in Rochdale where they train Freestyle Dancers.

The Joys of Dance. (Reproduced with kind permission of the artist Stephanie Jones)

In fact, they teach hundreds of children Freestyle and Street Dance, the result being that at the time of printing all of their teams hold British titles
- They also teach Social Ballroom, Latin American, Argentine Tango, Tap, and so on and so forth
- Teams trained by Stephanie and Steve have appeared on the BBC's *Come Dancing*, on *Blue Peter*, and more recently in the semi finals of *Britain's Got Talent*
- Whilst Stephanie keeps her hand – or should it be feet – in the dancing world, her other career as an artist is now going from strength to strength
- She paints dancers by commission, primarily in oils and pastels; her own practical dance expertise has given her an eye, insight and appreciation of the dance form, and indeed the dance world, that she would perhaps otherwise not have had
- In 2009 I invited Stephanie Jones to paint the front cover and illustrate the text for this book, *The Pocket Guide to Ballroom Dancing*, and although one can never be pleased at another's misfortune, that particular silver lining wasc ertainly over my head
- Early in 2010, on 7 February, along with her husband Steve, Stephanie won her second Carl Alan Award, which this time was a Lifetime Achievement Award
- As for her son PM, he went on to represent Britain in Latin American dancing at the World Championships before changing direction to become a commercial dancer and Musical Theatre artist; and as one would expect from this talented family, he has enjoyed success in that area too appearing on stage both in this country and on the Continent – I wonder if he can paint?

WELL, I NEVER KNEW THAT!

- Have you ever heard the term '*Cake Walk*' and wondered where it came from? Well, it originated in the late 1800s when the *Jive* was a competitive dance, and the prize was a cake, the result being that the *Jive* was then sometimes known as the *The Cake Walk*
- The BBC televised the popular programme *Come Dancing* from the Tower Ballroom, Blackpool for many years. More recently the BBC television programme *Strictly Come Dancing* also broadcast one of its programmes in the seventh series from the Tower Ballroom.

Anyone can Dance. (Reproduced with kind permission of the artist Stephanie Jones)

- Bruce Forsyth was evacuated at the start of the World War II, but was so homesick that he returned home just three days later
- In its first three series alone, *Strictly Come Dancing*'s contestants used a staggering 169 bottles of fake tan
- Bruce Forsyth's great-great-great-great grandfather, William Forsyth, was a founder of the Royal Horticultural Society and the namesake of the Forsythia plant
- The Tango was originally in the Latin American category of dancing, whilst the Jive was in the Ballroom category. However, they have now swapped places, the reason for this being that the Jive was the only Ballroom Dance that was danced out of hold, whereas the Tango was the only Latin dance that wasn't free, and so it made sense for the two to swap places
- Most people have heard the name Victor Silvester, but few know why he was given the name Victor – until now maybe. Apparently, it was because he was born on the very date that Mafeking was relieved during the Boer War – hence the name 'Victor'!
- During World War II and in 1941 BBC radio began broadcasting a show called *The BBC Dancing Club* in which there was a section featuring a dancing lesson with the steps being dictated by Victor Silvester. After he had finished there was a pause so that the listeners could write down the lesson – how quaint! Then it was discovered that these pauses were being used by Lord Haw Haw (William Joyce) to broadcast German propaganda. He was thwarted though by Victor repeating his instructions, rather than pausing
- On a windy day, if you happen to be at the top of Blackpool Tower, you can feel it paying homage to the dancers it frequently hosts as it sways slightly (a bow, perhaps) – and a little scarily too – in the wind. Let's just hope that it sticks with the 'rise', and ignores the 'fall', eh?
- Hanging above the Tower Ballroom in Blackpool are large crystal chandeliers which can be lowered to the floor for cleaning. This cleaning process takes more than a week
- At Fred Astaire's screen test it was famously said of him: 'Can't sing. Can't act. Can dance a little.' How wrong can the so called experts be!
- Dancesport is now recognized by the International Olympic Committee and so is an Olympic event. Quite right too!

- There are several dancers who have been honoured by the Queen for their services to dance
- In 1937 the Skating System for competitors' marks was introduced at Blackpool, (Ballroom), and this is still used today not only at Blackpool but all round the world too
- *Damsel in Distress* (1937) was the only film made by Fred Astaire that lost money at the box office
- In the 1950s a dance band was made up of 14 musicians – one on violin, four on rhythm, four on saxophones and five on brass
- The last dance of a social event evening, and referred to as just this – 'The Last Dance', is usually a Waltz
- In its original form the *Charleston* was a very wild dance and as a result many rather enthusiastic dancers were injured on the dance floor. This gave rise to that well-known slogan 'Please *Charleston* Quietly'
- The beautiful and stylish *Viennese Waltz* was banned at the turn of the nineteenth century because it was considered to be decadent
- It is said that if you can dance the *Foxtrot*, then you can dance any dance, for its simplicity is what makes it so difficult
- Prior to appearing as head judge on *Strictly Come Dancing*, Len Goodman appeared as both a dancer and a judge on the original TV show *Come Dancing*
- The dance craze *the Twist*, which arrived in the 1960s was the first partner dance in the new wave of dances in which no one touched each other, which in itself is bizarre as this was supposedly the decade of 'free love' and was, again supposedly, 'touchy feely' in the extreme
- Dancing is as old as mankind itself and there is evidence of this in the form of drawings made by prehistoric man of men and women dancing together. Some of these drawings can be found on the wall of a cave in Cogul, Northern Spain
- When *Strictly Come Dancing* first started there were two series per year; maybe there is only one now because they are afraid that they will run out of willing celebrities?
- Len Goodman, the head judge on *Strictly Come Dancing* actually became a professional Ballroom Dancer by default, it all came about when he injured his foot whilst playing football and was later told that his bones would never heal well enough for him to be a professional footballer and so he took up Ballroom Dancing instead

- Sadly many young men still think that Ballroom Dancing is a 'wet' pastime, yet Victor Silvester, as well as being one of the most famous Ballroom Dancers of all time, was also a decorated war hero
- The Cha-Cha is the most recent addition to the competitive Latin American dances
- Nelson Mandela mentions Victor Silvester's music as an inspiration during his many years in incarceration
- Most people now know that dancing is, as well as great fun, an excellent form of exercise, but just how many of you realize that it is actually more energetic than walking and that to dance a *Quickstep* for a mere 10–15 minutes is equivalent to walking for a mile?
- The name *Cha Cha(-Cha)* was given to the dance because it echoed the scuffing sound that the girls' feet made on the dance floor
- It was Victor Silvester who coined one of the oldest and best-known dance catchphrases: 'Slow, slow, quick quick, slow'

BIBLIOGRAPHY

REFERENCE BOOKS

Allen, J, *The Complete Idiot's Guide to Ballroom Dancing* (Marie Butler-Knight, 2002).

Bottomer, P, *Let's Dance* (Lorenz, 1998).

Du Beke, Anton, *Anton's Dance Classes* (Kyle Cathie, 2007).

Howard, G, *The Technique of Ballroom Dancing* (IDTA, 1987).

Irvine, B and B, *The Dancing Years* (WH Allen/Virgin, 1970).

Maloncy, A, *Strictly Come Dancing: The Official 2009 Annual* (BBC, 2009).

Silvester, V, *Dancing is My Life* (Heinemann, 1958).

, *Modern Ballroom Dancing* (Ebury, 2008).

Wainwright, L with King, L, *Need to Know: Ballroom Dancing* (Collins, 2007).

Whitworth, TA, *Learning the Essential Sequence Dances* (TA Whitworth, 1997).

WEB SITES

www.britannica.com
www.themave.com/Astaire

INDEX